Praises for *Finding Life after*

"If you are looking at this book, you are going through unspeakable grief, or you know someone who is. What Nikki and Alice have written is a special gift—a book unlike any other. Its comfort, practical guidance, and inspiration come from their own suffering, loss, hope, and joy. Let them walk with you through grief and help you find hope and joy again, in a way only those who have lost a child can truly understand."

—*David Gregory,* New York Times *bestselling*
author of Dinner with a Perfect Stranger

"*Finding Life after Losing One*, with Nikki King and Alice Rampton, is tender, powerful, and wise. It brings light into the dark experience of parents losing a child and shares personal, healing guidance for any who are bereaved and those who love and support them. Written by two mothers who have lived through a child's death and learned powerful lessons about grief and grace, their book is a balm in Gilead and provides insightful, moving, and practical counsel on living with loss and finding wholeness after a child dies."

—*Sean Brotherson, PhD, professor and bereavement*
researcher at North Dakota State University

"Few life events can match the tragedy and profound grief stemming from the loss of a child. Nikki King and Alice Rampton have provided us with a book that is at once a moving tribute to their own loss and an inspirational guide to help others."

—*John Saultz, MD, professor and chairman at*
Oregon Health Sciences University Family Medicine

"A moving, inspiring, and significant work to help parents cope with unimaginable grief after losing a child. Nikki King and Alice Rampton speak from heartfelt personal experience, offering hope and healing to those who are desperately seeking a measure of peace."

—*DeAnne Flynn, author of*
The Time-Starved Family *and* The Mother's Mite

"This was the first book we read after losing our young son Colton. It was very helpful to have our feelings validated and let us know that the pain, thoughts, fears, and lows we were experiencing were normal. We would recommend it to other parents and family members who have experienced loss."

Matthew and Amanda Smith, parents of Colton and Clayton Smith

"Grief is an isolating experience. Hearing from others who know grief and are willing to share the story of their ongoing journey through grief can be extremely helpful. This book not only provides great information about the world of grief but also shares the experiences of several families that are on the journey. Hearing about what they have felt and what they have learned can help those new to grief realize that they are not alone."

Melissa Allen, bereavement coordinator,
Benton Hospice Service, Corvallis, Oregon

"In my work with families with critically ill children, I see families grieving the loss of a child when it is still fresh, raw, and devastating. I see the shock, the intense sadness, and the way each family grieves and copes in their own personal way. I love Nikki and Alice's book because it is the collective wisdom from so many families who have experienced the loss of a child. No family chooses this kind of loss, and each family story is unique, but I am thankful for those who have chosen to share their stories with the rest of us. May this book honor all of the children who are gone."

Christy Burch, guest services coordinator, Ronald McDonald
House Charities of Oregon and Southwest Washington

finding life

after LOSING ONE

a parent's guide
for when a
child dies

NIKKI KING
& ALICE RAMPTON

an imprint of cedar fo

ISBN 13: 978-1-4621-1785-7

Published by Plain Sight Publishing, an imprint of Cedar Fort, Inc.,
2373 W. 700 S., Springville, UT 84663
Distributed by Cedar Fort, Inc., www.cedarfort.com

LIBRARY OF CONGRESS CATALOGING-IN-PUBLICATION DATA
King, Nikki, 1983- author.
 Finding life after losing one : a parent's guidebook for when a child dies / Nikki King [and] Alice Rampton.
    pages cm
 Includes bibliographical references.
 ISBN 978-1-4621-1785-7 (perfect bound : alk. paper)
 1. Children--Death--Psychological aspects. 2. Parents--Psychology. 3. Bereavement--Psychological aspects. I. Rampton, Alice, 1950- author. II. Title.

 BF575.G7K535 2015
 155.9'37085--dc23

                                    2015032441

Cover design by Lauren Error
Cover design © 2016 by Cedar Fort, Inc.
Edited and typeset by Eileen Leavitt

Printed in the United States of America

10 9 8 7 6 5 4 3 2 1

Printed on acid-free paper

This Book Is Dedicated To

Emma Joy Bradshaw
Dustin Guy Eichelberger
Dallan James Fisher
Megan Elaine Forrest
Marc David Harris
Troy Leonard Juntunen
Taylor Michelle King
Hannah Marie Kingsley
Elena Marie Knight
Sam Lahr
Craig Averill Leman
Lane Anthony Martin
Jackson McNutt
Cameron Merrill
Scott Frederick Merten
Lindsay Renee Miller
Lynette Lorane Miller
Joshua Roland Nelson
Wendy Lynne Nielsen
Jason Alan Newcomb
Alex Newport-Berra
Lora Dorothea Rampton
Brooke Carol Wilberger

CONTENTS

— ᥤ —

ACKNOWLEDGMENTS

Writing this book was a team effort. We could not have completed this project without the help of many individuals.

We would like to thank those who helped us with editing the book. First of all, Heather Schnese, who made wonderful suggestions about how to arrange the chapters. Her skill as an editor combined beautifully with her added vision of the book. We also appreciate dear friends and families who read the manuscript and found errors and punctuation problems that we missed entirely. They included Angeli Butler, Lisa Rampton Halverson, Judy Juntunen, Diane Merten, Rebecca Morris, Pat Newport, Cindy Rafn, and Tiffany Smith. Kevin Taylor compiled our resources and notes and did so with such diligence and exactness. We are thankful to Dr. Sean Brotherson, who brought his wealth of research and information to the book on the subject of grief. Kudos to photographers and friends Cherie Martin and Chris Becerra for their photos.

The message of this book is "You are not alone." Our contributing parents who added their poignant thoughts and insights reminded all of us that we were not alone. We are so grateful that they took the time to share the things of their hearts. Thank you, Caitlin Bradshaw, Debora Eichelberger, Susan Fisher, Elaine Forrest, Janet and Brent Harris, Judy Juntunen, Nadine Nielsen King, Brenda and Gary Kingsley, Candida Marie Knight, Ann and Mike Lahr, Craig and Nancy Leman, Karen Martin, Crystal McNutt, Cressey and Shelley Merrill, Greg and Diane Merten, Shanna Miller, Beth Nelson, Gina Newcomb, Pat Newport, Mark Rampton, and Cammy Wilberger. By sharing their messages, they had to revisit that time of grieving, and that is not an easy thing to do.

We thank Cedar Fort Publishing and their warm and professional staff for having faith in this book and recognizing that it has the potential to help those parents experiencing the greatest loss of all.

Last but not least, we thank our husbands, Eric King and Mark Rampton, who are our best friends and forever partners. You were there for us every step of the way, encouraging, loving, and supporting. We love you!

— ❧ —

PREFACE

Dear friend,

We wrote this book because of two little girls named Taylor and Lora. Neither of them lived to their second birthday. Born twenty-six years apart, they likely wouldn't have known each other, but we, their mothers, crossed the generations to write this book together.

For parents who have lost a child, this book is for you and your friends and family members. We know the loss of a child is unique, and we also know it's an unnatural occurrence for all parents. It is often said that parents should never have to experience the death of their child. We are meant to go first, not our children. And when a child dies, one of our greatest yearnings is for that unrealized future.

This book is designed to be a practical help to parents during the most difficult time of their lives. We incorporated our personal thoughts and experiences, along with those of more than twenty other parents who have lost a child. The ages of these children range from one day to forty-five years. The profound thoughts from other parents can be found at the end of each chapter. The children who inspired this book have short bios and photos, which can be found following chapter 14.

We hope you will use this book like a textbook for the school of hard knocks. Make it a survival manual for your grief. Highlight the paragraphs that touch your heart. Write in the margins. Cross out things that don't make sense to you. Jot down your personal thoughts and reflections at the end of the book.

Death takes many forms: overdose, suicide, accident, disease, murder, and the unknown. We don't pretend to understand the emotions or experiences of all parents who have lost a child; we wrote this book based on our own personal journeys. You didn't sign up for this experience, but you are now part of a group of parents who have a unique story to share. We hope this book offers comfort in knowing that you are not alone.

Love, Alice and Nikki

Alice Rampton   *Nikki King*

We begin with our own stories.

NIKKI

July 27, 2012, was a beautiful Oregon summer morning. After my four kids had eaten breakfast, we cleaned the house together and played a board game. Taylor, my sixteen-month-old, was always getting into anything she could, so I kept her occupied by chasing her around. I took my afternoon rest time while Tyson (seven), Natalie (five), and Alivia (three) played in their rooms. I needed my "Mommy time" to rock and nurse Taylor in quiet. It was my chance to unwind for a few minutes and just enjoy her baby stage.

The whole week prior, as I took the time to rock Taylor, I would get an overwhelming feeling to look her over, smell her, kiss her, and hold her close. I felt like someone was whispering in my ear, "Take every ounce of her in because she won't be here much longer." I kept thinking, *She's a baby. She's always with me. Where is she going to go?* Finally, I reasoned with myself that it didn't hurt to take the time to breathe her in and study every little finger and toe. So I did. That day, our family members were gathered from all over the Pacific Northwest for a reunion. It was always a fun time with family: food, games, and kids running around. I was going dancing that evening with my husband, Eric, and some family members. I was elated. I loved to dance, and getting away for the night is a treat for any mother of four little children.

After a fun day of playing outside, it was time to take the kids to a neighbor's house to be watched for the evening. I had brought Taylor inside the house and was going to get her and her siblings ready for the babysitter. Unknown to me or anyone else in the house, Taylor had gone to the front door and somehow managed to dart outside. Eric went to pull the car, which was backed in, out of the driveway because we were going to leave soon. Thinking that Taylor was safe inside, he moved the car forward, and that's when Taylor was hit by the right front tire. She was too small to be seen from the driver's seat. I heard commotion outside, and someone said that there had been an accident.

Eric's uncle, who was outside, heard a thump and saw Taylor. He immediately pulled her out from under the car. Eric came running into the house in a panic and screamed to call 911 and for someone to give him a towel.

There were at least eight people in the kitchen (including me), but no one said a word. No one handed him a towel. No one knew what had happened. Everyone just froze. My husband didn't wait for my frozen state to thaw. Eric grabbed a towel and raced back into the car and rushed our precious daughter to the emergency room. Their only thought was to get her there so she would be OK. Once in the emergency room, they laid the baby down on the gurney as gently as humanly possible.

Meanwhile, back in the kitchen, it took probably a few moments for everyone to jump into action, though it felt like it had been hours. A cousin had gone outside to see what was happening when Eric had rushed in the door. Once my husband left, she told me that Taylor had been hit. Immediately, I shook my head and said, "No, it's not true!" I wasn't ever going to believe that this had happened. It simply could not be what happened. I refused to believe it. But there is something that happens inside you when there is an emergency, and you need to react. I short-circuited. My body couldn't move. I simply couldn't process the information.

Then I saw Natalie race inside, wailing Taylor's name. She looked like she had seen a ghost. She had been outside playing with some dogs at the time Taylor was hit. She had seen her sister under the car. That scene is nothing an adult should ever see, let alone a five-year-old. I grabbed her and held her as close as I possibly could. I tried to process all that was happening around me. My two other children came from playing with their cousins downstairs and immediately knew something was wrong. I threw my arms around them and held all three. The other two had not seen the accident, but they were crying and frightened due to all the commotion. Amazingly, Natalie started singing songs she had learned in Sunday School at church. I began to rock all three kids and sing with Natalie, hoping it would calm down these frightened children.

Probably ten minutes later the phone rang, and I was told I needed to come to the hospital right away. I asked a family member to watch the kids, and I rushed to the hospital. Upon arrival, I was escorted into a room where Eric and other family members were waiting. They all looked awful. Eric was hysterical and kept saying, "I'm sorry. I'm sorry."

We stayed in that room for what felt like a lifetime. Then the doctor came in and said that Taylor had died on impact. They had tried everything possible to save her but were unsuccessful.

We lost it. I had never cried like this in my whole life. Eric was a mess and kept repeating, "Please don't blame me" and "I'm sorry. I'm sorry" over and over again. I gathered all the strength I could find and looked Eric in the eye and said, "I will never blame you if you never blame me." Eric wasn't the only one feeling guilty. As Taylor's mother, I felt I should have known she had gone outside toward the car.

I knew I had to go home to tell the children that their sister was gone. That was the most difficult thing I've ever had to do. They were sleeping, but the second I laid down next to Natalie, she woke up and asked, "Mommy, is Taylor going to be OK?"

Through tears, I had to say, "I'm sorry, sweetheart. She's gone." I couldn't say any more than that. We just held each other and cried until sleep overcame us. In the morning, we told the other children that she had passed away. Tearstained faces and heavy hearts became the norm in our house for many weeks.

Eric and I have stuck to the promises we made to each other that day. What we still struggle with today is the blame we place on ourselves. That's not helpful either. The reality is that our personal situation would only get worse if we lost each other as a result of this tragedy. Taylor was born because of our love, and together we strive to heal from this tragedy through our love.

ALICE

It was summertime—July 1985. We had moved back to Corvallis, Oregon (our hometown), twelve months earlier. Mark, my husband, had set up a solo family medical practice office; we had bought a home and were settling into life with our six children: Lisa (twelve), Meta (ten), Marcus (nine), Anna (seven), Sara (four), and baby Lora Dorothea (fourteen months). It had been a busy summer, with a family trip to Yellowstone.

Upon our return, the children had gotten a bug, and everyone seemed to have an upset tummy.

Lora's stomachache lasted longer than the others. She was irritable and acted uncomfortable. One afternoon, my sister, Linda Bryson, had come over to visit. We were sitting in the living room, and I was holding Lora, massaging her little stomach. In the process, I felt something hard and asked Linda to check it out. Linda had worked in medical offices, and she said, "You really need to have Mark check that out when he gets home."

When Mark came home, he immediately felt Lora's stomach. As he pressed into her abdomen, I saw a look of fear come over his face. He said that he was really worried because there seemed to be something that shouldn't be there. We called our pediatrician, and she arranged for Lora to have an abdominal ultrasound the next day. The ultrasound showed that there was a large mass on her left adrenal gland. An appointment was made for Lora to be seen at Oregon Health Sciences University in Portland. The doctors wanted to do a surgical biopsy. We were hoping that if it was a tumor, it would be something like a Wilms' tumor. Mark specifically said he did not want the diagnosis to be neuroblastoma, an often deadly pediatric cancer. I'll always remember the time we spent outside during her surgery, praying, hoping, and trying to prepare ourselves for whatever. We went back inside the hospital to await the results of the exploratory surgery. The doctor broke the news to us that they had opened up her abdomen and found that the tumor was too large to remove. It appeared to originate in the adrenal gland and had begun to invade her other organs. Surgery could've endangered her life, so they closed up the incision and decided to recommend chemotherapy to shrink the tumor.

This was not the diagnosis that we had prayed for and hoped for our little daughter. There really isn't any way to prepare yourself when the surgeons come out and tell you that the prognosis for a cure is very slim. She was given a 5 to 10 percent chance of survival. Our hearts were broken and heavy, but we moved forward to do whatever we could to keep our daughter healthy and alive.

A cancer treatment regimen was established for Lora, and we began driving the ninety miles for chemotherapy each week. When the result was not promising, Mark delved into his own cancer research. He spent hours reading and going to the library at Oregon State University to study all he could about neuroblastoma, possible breakthroughs, and so on.

This was prior to the Internet. Research was slow and tedious. He called other doctors he knew around the United States and even one in Hong Kong, trying to see if anyone was getting promising results in treating neuroblastoma. We heard about intraoperative radiation and surgery at Denver Children's Hospital in Colorado, which had some good results and seemed less detrimental than the full abdomen radiation, which was injuring Lora's organs. We went there in November 1985, and Lora went under the knife again. The doctors removed all of her growing tumor that was possible without injuring vital organs. The area with remaining tumor was directly radiated before closing up her incision. We were hopeful that this might work. She began to feel better and was eating more too.

At the same time, I was trying alternative methods of vitamins, heat, light, and music. When someone tells you that your child may die, you will do anything to try to prevent this from happening. Our Portland pediatric oncologist at the medical school was very negative about the prognosis. He simply felt that Lora would die. Yet every parent needs some kind of hope. Yes, the statistics were miserable, but a small percentage of children had survived. Why couldn't Lora be one of those who survived?

It was so difficult to balance the lives of our other five children with weekly chemotherapy treatments and various surgeries. We tried to make things as normal as possible, but nothing was normal. All of the children were praying nightly that Lora would get better and the cancer would go away. We still had piano lessons, ballet, homework, basketball, Scouts, and all the activities of Lora's siblings, but underneath it all, her cancer loomed large and ominous on our hearts and minds. Friends and family were an enormous help, but we had always been fairly self-sufficient, and it was hard to ask for assistance.

About a month after Lora's surgery in Denver, we packed up the family and drove to the ocean during the 1985 Christmas holidays. It turned out to be a beautiful day of sunshine, rare for December at the Oregon coast. We had a wonderful time as a family creating a Mickey Mouse sculpture, but we were sad when we realized that no one had brought a camera. (These were the days before smartphones.) We saw a man taking a walk on the beach and asked if he would take a family picture of all of us with our sand sculpture. He agreed to do this, and we told him we'd pay for film development and postage if he would mail us a copy of the photo. We gave him our mailing address, but we weren't too certain he would really come through with this request.

At the end of December, I took Lora to her local pediatrician for a checkup. She examined Lora, and when she pressed down on her abdomen, she shared the dreaded message that the tumor was back. I couldn't believe it! The surgery in Denver had removed nearly all the tumor and now it was back. It was such a fast-growing tumor. I had such a hate and abhorrence for cancer and all that it represented. Mark and I were devastated. Everything had been going so well, and we felt Lora had another lease on life, but this completely shut us down. By early January, the tumor filled her little belly once again. She continued to nurse, but she was very fussy about eating any other foods. I felt I could keep her alive by nursing her. But she had lost so much weight and was only fourteen pounds at twenty months old. She had weathered the chemo, radiation, and surgeries remarkably well, but now her eyes showed pain. She was not happy, and I knew that she was hurting.

On the night of January 8, 1986, Lora vomited some black bile. Mark said that her death might be imminent. She had lost so much weight, and we could feel the tumor bulging inside her abdomen. The feeling that she might die was oppressive. It was just too hard to accept. She'd been such a beautiful, healthy child. Our little daughter had a fun and mischievous nature and loved to get into things. She loved to dance. Her siblings adored and spoiled her. But now she was emaciated and unhappy. We had moved her crib into our bedroom so we could hear if she needed something. She slept through that night but awoke very early on January 9 and sat up in her bed, crying. I lifted her out of the crib and carried her in my arms to the diaper changer. Still cradling her in my arms on the changer, Lora simply reached up toward something and took her last breath. Mark came beside me, and we cried as we realized that she was gone.

We held her and softly cried and rocked her little body that was still warm. It was so hard to believe she had died. We awoke the other five children and brought them into the living room. It was early morning, and the sun was just beginning to rise. One by one, each of our children tenderly held Lora's little lifeless body in their arms and expressed their love for her. There was a beautiful peace in our home. After months of Lora having to feel pricks and pokes and pain, we knew she was at peace.

Grandparents and aunts also came and held her and said their goodbyes. Then it was time for the morticians to take her little, lifeless body. We wrapped her body in a blanket and gave her to the men from the mortuary. That was a difficult time. She would never again physically be in our home. Even though she was no longer inhabiting that body, it was still very hard to give her up. They were kind and gentle as they carried her, wrapped in a blanket, in their arms to their car in the driveway. But it seemed so final.

A couple of days later, we received a copy of the photo that was taken on that sunny, happy day at the Oregon coast. It turned out to be our last family photo with her. We will always be grateful for that merciful gift from a stranger walking on the beach.

1

IS WHAT I'M
FEELING NORMAL?

"Tonight all the hells of young grief have opened up again; the mad words, the bitter resentment, the fluttering in the stomach, the nightmare unreality, the wallowed-in tears. For in grief nothing 'stays put.' One keeps on emerging from a phase, but it always recurs. Round and round. Everything repeats. Am I going in circles, or dare I hope I am on a spiral?"[1]

—C. S. Lewis

A NEW AND CHANGING "NORM"

Extreme sadness, disbelief, rage, anger, regret, fear, hate, melancholy, disappointment, helplessness, numbness, hopelessness, vulnerability, self-pity, inability to concentrate, and lack of motivation are all emotions and states of being associated with grief. Those who have lost a child ride an emotional rollercoaster. What you're feeling is normal! Your whole world has changed—even the basics of your everyday life: eating, sleeping, and so on.

Life without your child becomes a "new normal." What is normal in this terrible, new reality? You may fluctuate between having no appetite to eating everything in sight, not sleeping to sleeping night and day, weeping constantly to not being able to cry, wanting to be with people to wanting to be totally alone, talking all the time to lacking energy to even complete a sentence. Although contradictory, all of these emotions are common and normal because grief is not straightforward—it's complicated and sneaky.

Losing a child is heartbreaking. And although the heartbreak is normal, it's unfamiliar and uncommonly painful. The pain can even seem unbearable at times. Some have described it as a warm knife in their heart, deep

1

and unlike anything that you have felt before. The losses are not one but many. Besides the death of your child, there may be the loss of identity, familiar routine, security, future expectations, or anything that has value or makes sense in life. Each loss hurts and each one is new to you.

— ✺ —

"When someone dies, it feels like the hole in your gum when a tooth falls out. You can chew, you can eat, you have plenty of other teeth, but your tongue keeps going back to that empty place, where all the nerves are still a little raw."[2]

Jodi Picoult

— ✺ —

How you deal with that loss and grief will be unique to you. Know that there is no right or wrong way to grieve, no appointed time to start, and no designated time to end.

Nikki: *Following Taylor's death, my husband slept about twelve hours a day instead of his normal six hours. This significant change in his sleeping pattern showed me how his body dealt with the heartache. As for me, I would walk the halls of our house in tears, sometimes all through the night. A few times, I didn't sleep for days. Food didn't look appetizing at all, though I knew I needed my strength more than ever. I remember getting upset at my husband for being able to sleep and wanting so much for that to be me, but we were just different.*

The way you hurt may look different from the way your spouse or significant other hurts. You may wear your emotions on your sleeve while your spouse holds them in, only to let them out in private. You may appear perfectly "normal" to others, while your spouse is a mess. Know that it's OK that your hurt will be unique and different from others.

TO CRY

For many people, crying is a natural part of grief. Tears are the body's natural release mechanism. Energy and feelings build up, and tears trigger a release. They are symbolic of the body saying that it is frustrated, overwhelmed, sad, or even just trying to get attention. Jodi DeLuca, PhD, a neuropsychologist at Tampa General Hospital in Florida, says crying can also be a survival mechanism. "When you cry," she says, "it's a signal you need to address something."[3]

Alice: *Mark and I experienced a type of crying that seemed almost like an animal wail. It was from as deep into the body and subconscious as one can go. It was primal and raw, low and involuntary. We lay in bed and cried this deep cry together. Weeping is not the word that describes this cry. We haven't experienced it since. Luckily, my sister was a counselor and explained to me that it was OK to cry in this way. It helped when someone was able to reassure us that something so seemingly unusual was totally normal.*

— ❧ —

"Crying is a natural emotional response
to certain feelings, usually sadness and hurt."[4]
Stephan Sideroff, PhD

— ❧ —

Nikki: *Let me tell you how irrational grief can make you. The day after my daughter died, I decided I was going to go into her room and make myself grieve. By doing this, I would accept this new reality. I figured if I immersed myself in her space and her belongings that I would deal with her death, right then and there, and get over it. Oh, how silly this sounds now. I did go into her room, for just a second, before I raced out of there. I couldn't stand the sight of the diapers she wouldn't be wearing or the bed that would stay empty. I didn't want to see the toys that she had just played with the day before. I couldn't handle her clothes sitting on the shelves, knowing she wouldn't wear them again. My heart ached. I cried a cry that I had never heard before. My body was shaking, and my legs gave out. Crouched down outside my daughter's bedroom, I cried harder than I have ever cried in my life. I'm not sure how long I cried, because I had no sense of time during the first few days of our tragedy. During this phase of continual crying, time was suspended. In fact, time was irrelevant. It's almost as though you go back to a stage of childlike innocence, when nothing matters in life except your emotions.*

— ❧ —

"The emotion that can break your heart is
sometimes the very one that heals it."[5]
Nicholas Sparks

— ❧ —

There are days when you cry until you feel you have no tears left. You may be a weepy mess one day and just fine the next day. There are days when you may feel like there is a cloud or dense fog surrounding you. There may even be days when you feel nothing. You may forget your loss for a brief period of time. Numbness can set in and last for days, weeks, or months. There may be guilt that comes with this numbness. If you can't cry, don't beat yourself up; it doesn't mean that you are without pain. Your body may just be giving itself the rest it needs to get through this period of time.

There are no rules to be followed here. A variety of emotions—or an absence of emotions—may be part of each day.

Alice's journal entry, January 16, 1986: *"Some days I don't see how I can live a life on earth without Lora. The entire fiber of my body aches to hold her. I look at pictures of her and cry without control. It's too hard. It's too much to go through. I see babies her age and I cry. I go to a store and can barely push the shopping cart past the baby food section. On TV today, there was a program about cancer and all the cures, and I feel so bad thinking that maybe there was something that could've been done to save her. It's been a week now, and today was especially hard because a week ago we woke up to her dying in my arms. I miss her so much. The house is so quiet. I keep listening for her to cry. My milk is still in and there's no baby to nurse. I keep counting eight meals to fix. The other kids have needs to be met and I've centered in on them, but today I just feel so sad and am so tired of meeting everyone else's needs. I want to know where she is and what she is doing. Why couldn't I have just raised her?"*

GRIEF'S PHYSICALITY

Your hurt is physical. Your body and mind are under stress. There may be days when every part of your body aches, and these aches are symptoms of depression and grief. Headaches can be a result of grief. In fact, you may be dehydrated from crying so much. Weight loss or weight gain can be a sign of grief. Body temperature may fluctuate. Your metabolism and energy may increase or decrease. Any of these physical happenings could be the body's way of dealing with loss. Being aware of how grief can affect your body may help you deal with the many new symptoms that can result.

You may experience a hyper-awareness of what's important in life.

You may feel anger or irritation with having to deal with the mundane parts of living. Needing to rake leaves, wash dishes, gas up your car, go shopping—all of a sudden these needs become irrelevant and unimportant in life. You may wonder why these tasks keep happening when your child has just died. It doesn't fit or make sense. It's almost like you are experiencing the same kind of culture shock you may experience when visiting another country. This time the "other country" is your life. Misty Zeller, a "mommy blogger" (CharliesSong.Wordpress.com) who lost her son Charlie, states it this way: "And then . . . you bury a child. That precious child you had wanted. And every other suffering you've known before this . . . feels like you've spent your whole life splashing in a shallow kiddy pool by comparison. All you can do is pray that God is very slowly teaching you how to swim."[6] Nicholas Wolterstorff put it this way in his book *Lament for a Son*, "The world looks different now. The pinks have become purple, the yellows brown. . . . Something is over. In the deepest levels of my existence something is finished, done. My life is divided into before and after the death."[7] These are all very real thoughts and feelings that are normal to a grieving parent.

Alice: *I visited a friend who had just lost a beloved son in a mountain accident. This was a strong woman who had accomplished much in her life. As I wrapped my arms around her, the grief was palpable and consuming. She was beyond heartbroken. The loss and sorrow of a grieving parent has no match. It's almost indescribable. Later that night, I tried to think of a visual that fit those emotions. It was difficult. The closest image I could conjure was of a large, drenched towel. Have you ever had a large, thick beach towel get soaked in the ocean or lake? Not just damp, but soaked until it is heavy and too full of moisture to wring out the water? You can barely carry it because it's so bulky, heavy, and oppressive. Grief is like that. It's bulky, heavy, and oppressive. It weighs you down. You can't get your arms around it. It lays its wet, cold thickness on your shoulders and gives you a feeling of hopelessness that nothing will ever be the same.*

The depth of your emotions can leave you feeling ungrounded. In the movie *Gravity*, the main character had lost a daughter years ago and is struggling to move on. Later in life, as an astronaut, she is in a life-threatening situation in a space capsule, where she is quickly losing oxygen. She has basically given up on life when her colleague asks her some profound questions and then shares this message with her: "What's

TRY THIS
Close your eyes and picture yourself as a tree. The tree seems vulnerable to the whims of a storm. Now imagine you have roots growing out of your feet, and they are pushing into the ground. The roots travel deep into the soil. You begin to feel secure. The roots hold you safely in place. You are grounded, unmoved, and protected from the storm. You feel stronger and in control. Even for a moment.

the point of going on? What's the point of living? Your kid died. It doesn't get any rougher than that. Still, it's a matter of what you do now. . . . You've got to plant both feet on the ground and start living life."[8]

When you don't have control over the people or world around you, it may feel like you have lost your ground. Sometimes creating a visual image of strength can help you regain some of that lost ground.

Nikki: *When I feel the weight of the world on my shoulders, I imagine my clothes are all my issues, pain, and regret. Then, I picture my clothes falling off of me onto the floor. I step out and over them. I picture myself leaving all the disappointments and regrets behind me. Sometimes I actually take physical steps forward while doing this. I then imagine myself getting dressed in new, clean, comfortable clothes to start a new day, and I feel better.*

So not only is your heart broken, but you also might feel like your body, mind, and soul are broken too. Your whole being might react to such sadness, and you may hurt more deeply and painfully than ever imagined. Your hurt isn't just emotional; it's as deep as the atoms of which you are made. It all just hurts. Losing a child will likely be your toughest life experience. Although your grief and journey is your own, you are not alone in your pain, tears, and healing.

THOUGHTS FROM OTHERS WHO HAVE LOST A CHILD

"Grief is complicated. Most people don't understand that. Don't let others tell you how you should feel. Take all the time you need to walk the path. You will never be the same; don't let others try to make you be who you were before for their comfort. You now are faced with other losses in addition to the loss of your child. It's OK to grieve the loss of who you were before and the loss of other parts of your past life."

—Ann Lahr, mother of Sam Lahr (1989–2009)

"Cry! Crying is healing. It allows the body and soul to feel every emotion and to release the stress and pain. It heals the soul and the body."

—Debora Eichelberger, mother of Dustin Eichelberger (1985–2000)

"I never knew I could cry so much or hurt so deep. There's no way to prepare. Even though the feelings you feel are normal, they are far from your normal. Every day is so foreign in what is supposed to be the most familiar place—your life. I will never be the same. When he died, so did a piece of me. For me, getting to know the 'new me' feels so unnatural. So, enjoy the 'up' days when they come and try not to feel guilty for having them, because your child would want you to be happy. The 'low' days will come. Just ride them out the best you can."

—Shelley Merrill, mother of Cameron Merrill (2010–2013)

"It is true that time will heal. The first year was the hardest as we went through life's events such as the holidays and birthdays without him for the first time."

—Scott and Susan Fisher, parents of Dallan Fisher (1988–1992)

NOTES

1.   C. S. Lewis, *A Grief Observed* (New York: Bantam Books, 1976), 66–67.
2.   Jodi Picoult, *House Rules* (New York: Washington Square Press, 2010), 144.
3.   Jodi DeLuca, quoted in "Why We Cry: The Truth About Tearing Up," WebMD, accessed April 30, 2015, http://www.webmd.com/balance/features/why-we-cry-the-truth-about-tearing-up.
4.   Stephen Sideroff, ibid.
5.   Nicholas Sparks, *At First Sight* (New York: Time Warner Book Group, 2005).
6.   Misty Zeller, "In the Deep End," *Charlie's Song*, November 4, 2013, https://charliessong.wordpress.com/2013/11/04/in-the-deep-end/
7.   Nicholas Wolterstorff, *Lament for a Son* (Grand Rapids: Wm. B. Eerdmans Publishing Co., 1987), 46.
8.   *Gravity*, directed by Alfonso Cuarón (Burbank, California: Warner Bros. Pictures, October 4, 2013).

2

FUNERALS, OBITUARIES, AND MEMORIAL SERVICES

THINGS YOU NEVER WANTED TO KNOW

*"Sharing tales of those we've lost is how
we keep from really losing them."*[1]
—Mitch Albom, *For One More Day*

THE PRESSING DECISIONS

When you welcome children into the world, you dream of their futures. You think about what they will enjoy doing, who they will look like, and what contributions they will make to this world. Unless your child is born with a life-threatening situation, the last thought on your mind is how to take care of funeral arrangements.

Just as parents aren't given a golden spoon when it comes to parenting, we never think of needing to prepare for a child's death. But if your child dies, you will immediately need to make many decisions, which may include

- organ donations
- cremation, burial, interment, or other methods to take care of the remains
- type of casket or urn to purchase
- where to place the remains
- wording of the obituary
- memorial or funeral service plans
- people to notify

That is a lot to place on the shoulders of a grieving parent. The problem is that no one knew your child as well as you, the parent. Even if others take on many of these responsibilities, part of accepting your child's death is participating in these events.

Here are some additional actions and decisions that families who have lost a child may need to face within a short period of time—along with suggestions and tips:

If your child's death is expected, ask someone to help you remember to look at a clock so you know the time of his or her death. This will be required on their death certificate. Hospital personnel are prepared for this, but if your child dies at home, it might be missed.

Be prepared for a police report. A child's death is what the legal system terms as "untimely." Therefore, the police will be called whether the death was imminent and expected or accidental and a total surprise. This is necessary to rule out any foul play. Don't be upset at the intrusion by a police officer, if it happens.

Notify family members and close friends. They will want to know. This can be delegated to close friends or family members if you don't want to do it. Just provide them with a list of names and what you would like them to say. If details of the death are painful, then choose a person who will be sensitive and yet direct enough to let family know that further information will be provided at a later time.

Choose a cemetery or other location for a resting place.

Contact a funeral home. Most funeral home directors are wonderful when it comes to helping you with details. They have experience with the death of a child. They can help you with decisions that may include

- deciding between cremation, burial, or interment
- choosing an urn or casket
- opting for a viewing, open casket, or neither
- contacting the newspaper to place a notice of death (obituary can come later)
- deciding when and where to have a memorial service, funeral, or celebration of life
- choosing a grave marker, if applicable. This is not a decision that needs to be made quickly. The choice of a headstone or marker can be done at any time and does not need to be accomplished before a funeral.

Complete the necessary paperwork required for the death certificate and insurance. Depending on the cause of death, insurance may cover many items, including the cost of burial. Remember to make copies of anything that you send in the mail. Order more than one copy of the death certificate in case you need to send official copies to health insurance companies or other agencies.

Think about what you want in the obituary. Like inscriptions on grave markers, the obituary is a permanent record that your child lived on the earth. It's natural to want others to know your child, and the obituary can be an important final tribute. If you are not a writer, find someone to help write the obituary. Many people want to help in the aftermath of such a loss, and this is one way someone can be of assistance. Include the location, time, and date of a service. If the service is to be held at a later, unknown date, that can be simply stated in the obituary.

Individuals may want to make a monetary gift in memory of your child. Determine the recipient of that gift and include this information in the obituary. It may be a nonprofit organization, educational fund, service club, school, sports team, or something else who may have been dear to the heart of your family or your child. You can also allow donors to choose their own charity.

Pick a date for the service. Unless your religious beliefs suggest an immediate burial, this does not have to be rushed. You may wish to accommodate family members who may be far away. Picking the date will provide you structure during a very unstructured time of your life and give you a focus point on which to plan.

Alice: *Lora died on Thursday morning, shortly before 6:00 a.m., at our home. We kept her body with us for a few hours so her siblings could hold her one more time. Other family members also came by the house for their farewells. One of the hardest things was having her little body taken away. I'm grateful that they didn't put her in a body bag but simply carried her body to the car owned by the mortuary. Even though I had faith that her spirit had left her body, I still didn't like the thought of her little cancer-ridden shell being put into a mortuary cooler. It seemed unnatural. We also knew that some friends and family had plans for that Saturday, so we decided to hold the memorial service the next day, on Friday afternoon. Planning the memorial service was a blur. We had to rush to choose a casket, a grave, her burial clothing, and so on. Friends were there to help, and one special couple even provided her with a beautiful gown in which to be buried. One friend came at the drop of a hat to sing a solo at the service.*

In the end, all went fine, but it was just too rushed. The newspaper notice of her death was not published until the morning of the service. Many friends told us later they were so sad to miss the service, because they did not know she had died. These are things we can never do over again. If I were to do her service over, I would wait until Saturday. My daughter only dies once. Prioritize what you and your family need at this time, not what others need.

Memorial Service or Celebration of Life

Whether you call it a memorial service, funeral, or celebration of life, this event is a time to reflect on your child as a person who lived on this earth, whether for seconds or for years. Some well-intentioned friends or families may try to make this event as complicated as a wedding celebration, but it's not a show. Simplicity at this time of your life will be more conducive to healing than being burdened with details that weigh you down. If some details are just too difficult for you to manage, delegate them to someone else.

You may want to consider the following for a funeral or memorial service:

- music
- life stories and speakers
- slideshow or presentation
- programs to pass out
- flowers
- photographs
- items that represent your child's life and personality
- guest book

If you are working with a funeral home or church, synagogue, or mosque, they will likely be aware of these details. If you are planning a service without professional guidance, there may be additional things to remember, like easels, tablecloths, projectors, screens, and baskets for cards. Do you want a meal for the extended family members following the service? Has someone been assigned to take photos? Will you bring flowers from home or will some be provided? Have you considered releasing balloons after the gathering?

There is so much to think about. Use friends and family to help lift your burden. Sit down with those close to you and discuss your needs and wants to make the service meaningful. Tell the right person if you feel strongly that you want a particular thing to happen. Don't let these details weigh you down. People want to help. This is the time to accept their support.

THOUGHTS FROM OTHERS WHO HAVE LOST A CHILD

"We had a 'Celebration of Life' service. Even though we were hurting and grieving, we wanted to make sure that Hannah's life was celebrated and God was honored for the precious gift He had given us. We asked people to wear bright colors. Hannah's favorites were pink, purple, and yellow. We wanted the service to be appropriate for children of all ages, in content and time. We did not have a casket at the service; instead we had several enlarged pictures of Hannah, her huge teddy bear, and flowers. Our oldest daughter, Meagan, made a DVD of Hannah's life with background music of two songs: 'Cinderella' by Steven Curtis Chapman and 'Wish You Were Here' by Mark Harris. The guest book was a scrapbooking book. Pages were decorated and laid out on tables for friends and family to write messages or memories or just sign. Some friends and family also got up at the end of the service and shared their thoughts. We feel like we celebrated Hannah's life and God. We wouldn't change anything."

—Brenda Kingsley, mother of Hannah Marie Kingsley (2004–2009)

"I gave the eulogy and I am still glad I did. I knew him and his story. I did write it out, as I wasn't sure how I would be able to handle my emotions as I talked about my son. It was an opportunity for me to express my feelings about Dallan and to make a public farewell. We placed a picture of Dallan on the casket. I had a single red rose that I laid on top of his casket when it was buried as a symbol of our love for him. It was one of the hardest things I have ever done to walk away from his casket on that cold, wintry day."

—Susan Fisher, mother of Dallan Fisher (1988–1992)

"We were blessed to have a lovely service when Lynette died. The word went out to folks to wear some yellow to honor Lynette, as that was her favorite color. I still remember looking around and seeing all of those pops of yellow. A thoughtful friend purchased some yellow ribbon and she, her husband, and adult stepsons made yellow ribbons for people to wear at the service."

—Shanna Miller, mother of Lindsay Miller (1978–1978) and Lynette Miller (1981–2011)

"I picked the music that said what I wanted it to say, even if was nontraditional. We served Sam's favorite foods at the reception (hot dogs, Mountain Dew, animal cookies, and so on). I'm really happy I did *not* have an open microphone. Instead, I had nice paper and pens at the reception on which his friends could express their thoughts and feelings. These pages were then assembled into a scrapbook."

—Ann Lahr, mother of Sam Lahr (1989–2009)

"The display we had about Josh's life for people to look at before and after the funeral was good for us to put up, as well as for people to see. A nephew quickly made a slide show with lots of pictures, and that was great to have as well. The one disappointment was that the service wasn't recorded."

—Beth Nelson, mother of Joshua Roland Nelson (1992–2012)

"In the memorial announcement, I had a poem enclosed that expressed my feelings about always being too busy and not concentrating on the important things. There were musical numbers that meant a lot to me. The funeral director made sure that dandelions that Lane's friends had brought to me were in a vase and on the pulpit where everyone could see them. I had 'Lane's Legacy' written on his grave marker."

—Karen Martin, mother of Lane Anthony Martin (1971–1982)

"Our doctor was kind enough to recommend a resting place and a funeral home. The service was in accordance to what he would have wanted; it was not designed to meet my needs or expectations, and so it was right. Do what is in your heart to do."

—Gina Newcomb, mother of Jas Newcomb (1980–2005)

"I loved Megan's service and was happy with everything. We invited speakers who had a relationship with Megan and knew and loved her. We played Billy Joel's 'Lullaby' and displayed all of her teddy bears. We also had a display of her life and other things that she loved. My mother had made a white dress, and that was what we wanted to bury Megan wearing. My mom was ill and unable to attend the funeral, so we felt a part of her was there."

—Elaine Forrest, mother of Megan Forrest (1985–2005)

"Gary and I decided on burial. It was one of those things we didn't discuss much. There are only two cemeteries, one in the middle of downtown Anchorage and the other on the outskirts of town, so it wasn't a hard decision. We chose Angelus, the one on the edge of town. It's beautiful and well kept. Hannah was an organ donor, so on the marker we put the organ donor medallion, the meaning of Hannah's name: 'God's gracious gift,' and verses that have meant a lot to our family: Proverbs 3:5–6."

—Brenda Kingsley, mother of Hannah Marie Kingsley (2004–2009)

"It was my decision that—after all of the medical procedures, poking, prodding, needles, medications—his body had been through enough already. So I decided no embalming, nothing. Just favorite clothes, a special blanket I had made for him, an ankle bracelet that Emma (our daughter) made for him, and his favorite book were placed with him in his casket, and that was enough 'processing.' His marker says, 'Gift of God.' We all feel he was a gift to us; he taught us so much. It was fitting. He was and is God's gift to us."

—Gina Newcomb, mother of Jas Newcomb (1980–2005)

"There are certain words I still cannot say, after ten months . . . and I realize I don't have to say them or listen to them. Die, death, funeral, obituary. They are too final. Instead of a memorial service, we had 'Gatherings to Honor Alex.'"

—Pat Newport, mother of Alex Newport-Berra (1981–2014)

"Sam had a favorite beach, and it made sense to cremate him and put his ashes in the ocean. After seeing his body in a body bag we just couldn't face a coffin."

—Ann Lahr, mother of Sam Lahr (1989–2009)

"When Wendy died, we were living in Western Samoa. Embalming was not done there, and we were required to bury her within twenty-four hours, so we did not have many options. I had just given birth to a baby son and was released from the hospital after our daughter had died. Wendy was buried on our church's property, next to another child who had died in 1924. A small marker was placed on her grave. Later, in 1993, we returned with a headstone to be placed on her grave."

—Nadine Nielsen King, mother of Wendy Lynne Nielsen (1960–1961)

"There is some solace in visiting the grave, even when you know they aren't there. We wanted the grave marker to be personal, so we designed it ourselves. We chose to put a train on the marker because our son loved trains. His name, birth date, and death date were all incorporated into the train etching. There is also a poem around the marker's edge, adapted from an original written by Sheri Bird. It says, 'Although you stand at my grave and weep, I am not here, I do not sleep. I walk on heaven's golden streets and listen at my Savior's feet.' We added pictures of Shamu the whale and Bambi and signed it with love from my husband and me. We had also put his siblings names. I just didn't think of that until one of them mentioned it."

—Susan Fisher, mother of Dallan Fisher (1988–1992)

"We decided to have the family decide together where Megan was to be buried. We visited all of the cemeteries and just felt that Locke Cemetery was the place. It took about a year for us to find the right marker. I wanted a teddy bear on the stone, but all of them were for newborn or toddler markers. After a year, I found one that was just right. We also had 'Goodnight, My Angel' engraved on the marker as it was from Billy Joel's song. We chose the prettiest casket. It wasn't cheap, but we decided that we would never get to help pay for Megan's wedding or college. I don't have any regrets, and that's important."

—Elaine Forrest, mother of Megan Forrest (1985–2005)

"Our two oldest sons wanted to speak at the funeral of their younger brother, and both did really well. It seemed appropriate for my husband, Greg, and me to stand together to express appreciation for all who came and had traveled so far. Three years earlier, my sister, Doris, had died, and a counselor suggested that I write a letter to Doris. We decided to invite Scott's friends to write something and send it to us. We received many letters from not only his friends but also several teachers, some addressed to Scott. We treasure these letters."

—Diane Merten, mother of Scott Merten (1973–1990)

"It took my husband, Greg, and me more than three years working with a very patient mortuary stonecutter to finally come to a decision about the final grave marker for our son. Greg was incredibly understanding of my emotional crisis and at one point just told the stone cutter that we would eventually be back. Two years later, I was finally ready to complete what we had started. I love cemeteries and have been putting flowers on family graves since I was a small child. But somehow, the finality of putting a grave stone on my own child's grave was something I had to struggle with and mature into before it could happen."

—*Diane Merten, mother of Scott Merten (1973–1990)*

"I had a really close friend take a few pictures from the service. At the time, I had no idea if I would ever look at the images. Then a few weeks after the service, I did open them up and look through them. There are images and words that will never fade from my memory while other entire segments are missing. Now, as I look at the pictures of the service, I am relieved that someone took the time to make this visual documentation. That difficult day is a part of my history, and I have those pictures as a record. They aren't ones I often pull up, and I will never display them in frames, yet I have them. All our experiences shape us, and while I usually will linger on the cheerful ones, I think it is also import to reflect on the more solemn moments, which these pictures help me to do. My husband's grandparents had bought an extra plot for one of their daughters who never married. She offered it to us for our baby because we had never imagined needing to plan for a child's death. On her headstone we chose the three adjectives that best summarized her short but sweet five months with us: 'Happy, Beautiful, Lovable.'"

—*Candida Marie Knight, mother of Elena Marie Knight (2009–2010)*

NOTE

1. Mitch Albom, *For One More Day* (New York: Hyperion, 2006), 197

3

STAGES OF GRIEF

"Grief is the price we pay for love."[1]
—Prince William, Duke of Cambridge

FIVE STAGES

Elisabeth Kübler-Ross, MD, a Swiss-American psychiatrist, was one of the first professionals to study the grief process. Her 1969 groundbreaking book, *On Death and Dying*, identified the five stages of grief: denial, anger, bargaining, depression, and acceptance. Her book helped raise public awareness about what had previously been private. No longer did people have to wonder if they were the only ones feeling the deep, foreign emotions associated with grief. Kübler-Ross helped those grieving to find common experiences with others facing loss and recognize universal attributes.

Understanding these stages can help us prepare for the grieving process. Kübler-Ross and her colleague, David Kessler, took a closer look at these stages in their book entitled *On Grief and Grieving: Finding the Meaning of Grief through the Five Stages of Loss*. In chapter 1 they wrote, "The five stages—denial, anger, bargaining, depression, and acceptance—are a part of the framework that makes up our learning to live with the one we lost. They are tools to help us frame and identify what we may be feeling. But they are not stops on some linear timeline in grief. Not everyone goes through all of them or goes in some subscribed order."

These stages have stood the test of time for nearly half a century. Grieving parents around the world have found a common grief culture in these five stages.

17

Denial

Denial is often accompanied with shock. Together they create an overwhelming and unbelievable state of being.

The death of a child is traumatic and painful. The very essence of life is questioned after experiencing such a loss, and a person may wonder if he or she can even continue to live. Denial gives us the ability to cope in incremental steps. Our thought processes recount the loss over and over. We analyze and reflect on every circumstance associated with the death. We wonder if it could've been prevented, and if so, how? We question everything. As long as we can find another scenario of what might have been, we can deny that death occurred. Slowly reality takes over, and we begin to believe that the child is really gone. This is a step in healing, but it also allows feelings and emotions to emerge that were being suppressed.

Anger

This stage is important in the grieving process. Some of us have been taught to contain our anger and "stuff it away" lest it cause contention and discord. But to deny that we feel anger can have unhealthy consequences of a longer nature. We may feel anger toward everything—anger that the child is gone, anger at ourselves for not being able to prevent the loss, and anger at anyone who might've played some role in the loss. Sometimes we feel anger toward someone for no justifiable reason except that anger is a tangible entity that can be easily focused at someone or something. We may also feel anger toward God for not stepping in and preventing the death. We may think, *If God is all-powerful, couldn't He have stopped the death of our child?* All of these emotions and feelings are normal. Kübler-Ross and Kessler wrote, "Anger is a necessary stage of the healing process. Be willing to feel your anger, even though it may seem endless. The more your truly feel it, the more it will begin to dissipate and the more you will heal."[2]

It can be beneficial to talk to a counselor or trusted friends about the anger you are experiencing. Like a referee at an athletic event, they view the entire game, while we are stuck at the beginning. Don't negate the benefits that come from anger. It can stimulate an inner strength and ability to fight our way back to a healthier existence. Anger is a pathway from the denial stage as we begin to validate feelings that were suppressed earlier. Underneath our anger is a bevy of other feelings such as pain, helplessness, inadequacy, guilt, and loneliness.

As these are uncovered, you may realize that it all boils down to the pain of loss that is associated with a death of a child. The ability to love can run parallel to the emotion of anger. Though raw and messy, the anger will begin to subside if we don't deny its existence.

Bargaining

Haven't we all bargained sometime in our life? It may be with another individual or with ourselves or in a prayer to God. Think back to your childhood when you would skip over the cracks in a sidewalk so you wouldn't "break your mother's back." It may sound silly now, but there was a serious intent to skip the cracks to avoid some type of punishment or negative consequence.

Bargaining can occur at various times. If a child has been injured or is ill with a terminal disease, we may bargain with God, offering all types of promises, such as pleading that if the child survives, we will be a better parent in the future. We might even offer our own life in place of our child. Bargaining goes hand in hand with guilt and feelings of inadequacy. We spend a lot of time thinking of the "what ifs." After a death, grieving parents may bargain with God that if they live a certain way, they will be assured that no other children will be taken.

Most of the time, we recognize that the bargains may be actually beyond our control, but perhaps the act of bargaining gives us a sense of purpose and power for a period of time. As Kübler-Ross and Kessler explain, "Bargaining can help our mind move from one state of loss to another. It can be a way station that gives our psyche the time it may need to adjust. Bargaining may fill the gaps that our strong emotions generally dominate, which often keep suffering at a distance. It allows us to believe that we can restore order to the chaos that has taken over."[3]

Depression

Depression is not a sign that you are mentally ill. It is a natural reaction to the profound loss that you have experienced. This is the time when we may withdraw from our friends and family and do not find joy or purpose in many activities. The pain we feel is unmasked, deep, and real. We can't deny that pain, and we can't bargain it away. It's just there. Family and friends may feel concerned about this depression and want us to simply get over the death and feel fine again.

Kübler-Ross and Kessler provide good advice for all of us: "As difficult as it is to endure, depression has elements that can be helpful in grief. It slows us down and allows us to take real stock of the loss. It makes us rebuild ourselves from the ground up. It clears the deck for growth. It takes us to a deeper place in our soul that we would not normally explore."[4]

Clinical depression that continues without resolution and manifests as an excessively depressed state needs to be addressed by someone trained to make a correct diagnosis. This is covered further in chapter 7, "Heathy Healing."

Acceptance

Kübler-Ross and Kessler explain the stage of acceptance in this way, "This stage is about accepting the reality that our loved one is physically gone and recognizing that this new reality is the permanent reality. We will never like this reality or make it OK, but eventually we accept it. We learn to live with it. It is the new norm with which we must learn to live."[5]

Can our child be replaced? We all know the answer to that question. But our hearts and minds can feel joy and peace once again while still remembering that special person. With the passage of time, we may even be able to reach out to others who have experienced a similar type of loss.

— ❧ —

"We must be willing to let go of the life we planned
so as to have the life that is waiting for us."[6]

Joseph Campbell

— ❧ —

Pay attention to these five stages and their descriptions. By understanding them, you will better understand yourself and your emotions. These stages come and go; some last longer than others. You may find yourself in the anger stage and the next day in the denial stage. There is a reason they are called *stages* and not *steps*. You will not always experience them in the listed order, but you will likely experience each of these stages. Try to stay in touch with your emotions. When the grieving process starts, so does healing.

— ❧ —

"There will be many chapters in your life.
Don't get stuck in the one you're in."[7]

Ryanintheus.com

— ❧ —

Alice: *In 1977, I was living in Augusta, Georgia, with my husband, Mark, and three children. Mark was in his medical residency with no free time in his schedule. He received a notice that Dr. Elisabeth Kübler-Ross was going to be speaking at the Augusta College and asked if I wanted to go in his place. I remember attending her seminar entitled "Death is a Continuous as Well as a Final Stage of Growth," and being moved by her presentation. I have saved the seminar brochure, the newspaper clipping about the seminar, and my notes from the event for nearly forty years. At the time, she said there were only about thirty hospices in the United States caring for the terminally ill. Now, practically every city in our country has a hospice organization. Death back then was not discussed. It happened, and you dealt with it. Little did I know that within ten years of hearing her talk, I would have a daughter with a terminal illness. During that struggle, I turned to Kübler-Ross's books and found comfort in her words. Being aware of the stages of grief does not mean you won't experience grief; it simply means you'll have a little more understanding when it hits you.*

TRY THIS
Try to recognize the stage of grief you might be experiencing. Keep a journal and write down what might have brought you to that stage. Was it a memory? Was it something someone said? Become familiar with the stages because they may be associated with triggers. (See chapter 6.)

Nikki's journal entry (ten months after Taylor's death): *I feel like there is a time when we mature through our grief, much like we do from childhood to adulthood. Here is my analogy: We begin our grief as "a young child," only thinking about our own needs and bargaining to get our way. I was so wrapped up in my own self-pity that I couldn't see anyone else's pain.*

The next stage of maturity, "awkward preteen" phase, is feeling like your identity is solely based on losing a child. I felt my identity was as the mother who lost her child. Then you may hit the "rebellious teenage" phase of blaming yourself, God, or others.

The "mature adult" came when I realized that bad things happen to good people and that I may never know why this happened. I'm not quite there yet. I still continue to ask why this happened and why me and express that this isn't fair. Fair or not, it did happen, and now I must deal with it. Maturity comes when we acknowledge what happened and move forward.

We pay tribute to those early pioneers, like Kübler-Ross, who brought scientific study to the subject of grieving. Not only did they bring to light the various stages that we may experience, but they also provide us with a sense of comfort and unity, knowing that we aren't alone in this process.

THOUGHTS FROM OTHERS WHO HAVE LOST A CHILD

"It helps to recognize that there are definite stages of grief and that a person doesn't go through them sequentially. Some stages may be experienced simultaneously. It's normal for most parents who have lost a child to feel like they are going crazy at times."

—*Karen Martin, mother of Lane Anthony Martin (1971–1982)*

"Grieving isn't something you do and get through. It is a process for the rest of your life; it just gets more bearable, and the emotions are not as intense. Each person has to go through each stage of the grieving process; there's no way to avoid any stages—they just happen. My son was hit on his bike by a young woman in our community. At the time of the accident, when the Spirit of God was close beside me, I was able to forgive this woman. Then the anger stage hit, and every time I saw this gal with her family, it made me angry. I was angry that she still had a family unit intact.

"It took me a year to get through the anger stage toward this person and her family. One morning, I woke up and knew it was time to forgive again. It was Christmastime, so I had a flower arrangement sent to their home with a note from our family hoping for their family to be happy at this time of year. In the note I asked how their daughter was doing and wrote that I hoped she was doing well. After receiving the note and floral arrangement, their daughter came to our home and brought us a flower arrangement and asked how we all were doing. After that experience, I could face this family again."

—*Debora Eichelberger, mother of Dustin Eichelberger (1985–2000)*

"I don't think I was much help to my other children during the first year. They were resilient. Scott's younger sister, Anne, was once present when someone asked how the family was doing. I said that we felt we were on a roller coaster. Anne replied, 'But that's a good thing because we aren't all down at the same time.'"

—*Diane Merten, mother of Scott Merten (1973–1990)*

"I've read about grief and the reactions people have to losing a loved one, but I was surprised at how angry I was. I was angry because Troy died. I was even more upset when I found out that Troy had not done more to manage his health. As the months passed, the anger changed to sadness that he chose a path that may have shortened his life. I'm learning to be gentle with myself and that it is OK to grieve my way. I don't have to pay attention to people who tell me to move forward. I need to pay attention if I'm getting too depressed and need to find someone to talk to about my feelings. Most of all, I've learned that while the stages of grief have been outlined, there are no rules for grieving."

—*Judy Juntunen, mother of Troy Juntunen (1967–2012)*

NOTES

1. Prince William, quoted in "Prince William addresses Christchurch mourners," *Guardian*, accessed May 3, 2015, http://www.theguardian.com/uk/2011/mar/18/prince-william-addresses-christchurch-mourners.

2. Elisabeth Kübler-Ross and David Kessler, *On Grief and Grieving: Finding the Meaning of Grief Through the Five Stages of Loss* (New York: Scribner, 2005), 10–28.

3. Ibid.

4. Ibid.

5. Ibid.

6. Joseph Campbell, *Reflections on the Art of Living: A Joseph Campbell Companion*, ed. Robert Walter (San Anselmo: Joseph Campbell Foundation, 1991), 13.

7. Ryan Hodges, "Change by Chapters," *Ryanintheus*, March 23, 2015, http://www.ryanintheus.com/change-by-chapters/.

4

HOW LONG WILL THIS LAST?

"How complicated and individual mending is; the time required for healing cannot be measured against a fixed calendar."[1]

—Mary Jane Moffat

TIMELESS GRIEF

We often want answers that fit into neat, tidy boxes—black and white, hard and fast, linear and scheduled. But unfortunately, grief has no boundaries nor order and therefore no timeline. Yet anyone experiencing grief from the loss of a child wants to know how long it will last—*when* will it be over?

You will often hear the adages, "Time is a great healer" or "Time softens the blow." Does that mean you simply stop loving the person who has died? Do you just move on? Do you forget them? No. But it means that the pain lessens with time, and every waking moment is not spent remembering the child who has died. The scar remains, but it is not the deep, open wound of the past.

At the beginning you will likely be overwhelmed with memories and thoughts of your child. They may be present in all of your thoughts and dreams. These memories are seared into your subconscious. As the days and months and years go by, you may realize that your thoughts of that child are present but less frequent. Don't feel guilty. This is normal and is part of the process of healing.

Alice: *After Lora died, I had nothing to give to others beyond my immediate family. With five living children, it was all I could do to just keep up with laundry, schoolwork, piano lessons, sporting events, and so on. Fortunately, no one was expecting me to give any more, but I had grown up in a service-oriented family, and I felt my own dose of guilt by not giving to others in some way. I also knew that I felt good when I served in some manner in the community, helping out a neighbor, friend, or whomever. But my service bucket was empty. There was no desire to give or reach out to help someone in need. I felt numb and just did not have the capacity.*

I remember the exact day that changed. It was about six months after Lora died, and I was getting dressed to go somewhere. A friend, who I hadn't seen for years,

TRY THIS

If we are trying to get out of a deep, dark cave, most of us want to know how close we are to the entrance. When will we see light? When will we feel like exiting and joining the human race again? Ask a trusted friend or family member to go to lunch with you on a regular basis. This could be weekly, monthly, or as needed. Tell them how you are feeling and ask for their honest opinion. "Am I closer to the entrance, or have I backtracked further into the cave?" If the answer is always the latter, seek professional guidance.

called to tell me her son had drowned. She was very emotional and weeping on the phone. Her loss was fresh and deep. I found myself reaching out to her and trying to offer support and love. It came naturally. It felt good to look beyond myself. It was like a switch had been turned on. I felt an "out-of-body experience" where I was looking down at myself and seeing myself supporting someone else. I felt a peace and awareness that I was starting to heal. It was the beginning of being able to concentrate on something beyond my own grief and mourning. There is a Chinese proverb that comments on how we have to start with small steps, "The man who removed mountains began by carrying away small stones." For me, this experience of providing support to a friend was the first small stone I had been able to carry in a long time. I recognized it as the beginning of my healing.

— —

"People are like stained-glass windows. They sparkle and shine
when the sun is out, but when the darkness sets in, their true
beauty is revealed only if there is a light from within."
Unknown

— —

FOCUS ON *HOW* INSTEAD OF *WHEN*

Most of us have asked, "When will I be happy again?" But perhaps it can be more helpful to ask, "How can I accept this reality, and what can I learn from this experience?" There is no magic formula or definitive deadline when you can say that you are completely done with the grieving process. In fact, be wary when someone tells you that you should feel fine in so many days or weeks or months.

Nikki: *Twenty-eight months after my daughter died (two years and four months) I can genuinely say that I am happy and enjoy life again. I still miss my daughter, but I don't think of her as often as I used to. I think of her fondly and remember the good things. I can talk about her easily without tears. There are still days when something will trigger my emotions and I am knocked into a whirlwind of sadness, but those days are mostly gone. I am no longer consumed with thoughts of regret or sadness. I can control my thoughts and emotions. I took a walk yesterday and felt a great appreciation for the world around me. I wasn't thinking of all the bad in the world but of the beauty that surrounded me. I can be silly or goofy again and not feel guilty for it. I am genuinely enjoying life.*

Alice: *A friend encouraged me to attend a grief support group. At this meeting, I remember hearing a woman talk of the death of her daughter over twenty years prior. She did not weep, but I could tell that she still mourned her daughter's death. At the time, it seemed strange that she was dealing with this loss so many years after the event. It made me question if parents ever got over the death of their child. Was there no reprieve from the pain? Would it always pierce my heart? Would I always be on the verge of tears? I was frightened by that prospect. It's been over thirty years since Lora died. If I attended a grief support group today, the sadness and emotions would probably come to the surface. It may seem to others that I hadn't resolved the death of my* *child. I've learned that you never "get over" the death of a child. For me, it's impossible to say, "Lora died, but I can take her death and put it into a box and place it on the shelf and never again feel any pain or sorrow." Instead, Lora's death plays a large part in the definition of who I am today. But on a daily basis, I am fine. Time really does heal. The majority of my memories of Lora, now, are of her sparkle and spunk. I remember feeling guilty the first time I went an entire day and did not think about her. The emotions flood back, but there is no comparison to that fresh grief that is ever present at the beginning. Lora is loved and remembered, but now the majority of memories are joyful and natural.*

Take time to grieve. It is a normal emotion. Almost everyone who has walked the surface of planet earth has grieved in one way or another. You may not believe that the passage of time will help, but we can assure you that it will soften the blow. The overwhelming sadness will lessen with time. There is no magic formula to when this will happen. Don't feel guilty when the salve begins to work on your tender heart. Think of the healing as a gift.

— ❧ —

"You will feel better than this. Maybe not yet. But you will.
You just keep living, until you're alive again."[2]

— ❧ —

In the book *Death: The Final Stage of Growth* by Dr. Elisabeth Kübler-Ross, Roy and Jane Nichols are quoted: "The most beautiful people we have known are those who have known defeat, known suffering, known struggle, known loss, and have found their way out of the depths. These persons have an appreciation, a sensitivity, and an understanding of life that fills them with compassion, gentleness, and a deep loving concern. Beautiful people do not just happen."[3]

THOUGHTS FROM OTHERS WHO HAVE LOST A CHILD

"Grieving is definitely a process. It was years before I could really enjoy Christmas because the Christmas before he died was so sad. I would go through the motions for the other children, but my heart wasn't in it."

—*Susan Fisher, mother of Dallan Fisher (1988–1992)*

"I learned from Lane's death that one cannot compare losses. Each loss is unique. There are way too many variables to compare our own experiences, talents, coping mechanisms, family dynamics, and so on with another. It helped to know that this loss will always be a part of my life. The intensity of the loss subsides, but once you have carried and given birth to a child, the love and the expectations for his or her life will always be a part of you."

—*Karen Martin, mother of Lane Anthony Martin (1971–1982)*

"The greatest challenge in life is learning to thrive when things change for the worse. Elena's death forced us to give up an entire future that we never imagined we would have to relinquish. It meant we had to surrender our path and choose a new one, to keep our eyes forward, all the while learning to balance appreciation for what we were leaving behind and find hope for the path that was ahead. Today I remember what was: I remember my wiggly, happy, beautiful baby girl in our home. I remember that love was overflowing and how it wrapped us in a peaceful cocoon of our own making. Today I experience the full range of human emotion, understanding the splendor of its perfect moments and the agony of its trials, and find in the aligning of the two the deepest beauty of life. And today that is what holds us together and ties together our past, present, and future."

—*Candida Marie Knight, mother of Elena Marie Knight (2009–2010)*

"There isn't a right or wrong way to grieve; everyone does it in his or her own way. There also isn't a timeline when grieving stops. The pain and grief never fully go away; they just lessen over time and you learn to live with them. Accept the help that is offered, such as arrangements for the service, food, babysitting, and so on. You need to have some time to take care of yourself, especially if you have other children. Helping them work through their grief is necessary but may delay you working on yours, so take a little time. It's OK to do that."

—*Brenda Kingsley, mother of Hannah Marie Kingsley (2004–2009)*

"Our daughter, Hannah, was born with a heart defect. When she was six months old, she had a surgery that left her with a gaping chest wound. Her short life was hard. At age five, she had a stroke and died three days later.

"This gave us some time to prepare. We donated her organs. We planned a service. We entertained family who came to support us. We kept busy. It kept our minds off reality. The service came and went. Everyone went home. We were secure that Hannah was in heaven. Then, the pain set in. Hard pain. For me, the next twelve months are blank. I checked out. I went to work and I watched TV, and that's all I did. I interacted little with family and hardly at all with friends. I was not there for my family. I was depressed. It took a year to get out of that state. My family was very patient. I finally went to Grief Share, a program through a local church. Everyone had been telling me that I should be 'over' it by now. I learned at Grief Share that you never get over it—you just get through it. It is always there. Be reasonable, be humble, and take help from others when it is offered. Get healthy. Be patient. It gets better, but it takes time. It is now a part of me and defines me. I will never be over Hannah. At Grief Share, I found out that my grief was normal. Some people had been dealing with the loss for five months and some for five years."

—*Gary Kingsley, father of Hannah Marie Kingsley (2004–2009)*

NOTES

1. Mary Jane Moffat, quoted in "Miscarriage, Baby Loss," *Shelly King Therapy*, accessed May 22, 2015, http://www.shellykingtherapy.com/miscarriage-baby-loss.
2. *Call the Midwife*, episode 4, aired on 9 February 2014 (BBC One).
3. Roy and Jane Nichols, quoted in Elisabeth Kübler-Ross *Death: The Final Stage of Growth* (New York: Scribner, 1997).

5

THE GUILT AND "WHAT IFS"

"Guilt is a poisonous illusion. Many languages don't even have a word for guilt. Sure, we all feel it. But we also get to decide if we're going to let guilt bring us down or not. Acknowledge the feelings, and then give yourself permission to let them go."[1]

—Kris Carr

"The what-ifs and should-haves will eat your brain."[2]

—John O'Callaghan

THE DANGER IN LINGERING

"What if I had done something differently? Would my child still be alive?" For parents who have lost a child, the "what ifs" can be haunting.

- What if I had said no?
- What if I had driven slower?
- What if the cancer had been discovered earlier?
- What if I had been home?
- What if I had been more aware?
- What if I had followed that premonition to move to another city?
- What if I had locked up that gun?
- What if I had been a better parent?
- What if I had listened more?
- What if I had done something different during the pregnancy?
- What if I had recognized the signs of depression?
- What if I had made that phone call?

- What if I had said, "I love you."
- What if . . . ?

It's impossible not to ask the "what ifs." Often they'll replay over and over, leaving you exhausted. You may find yourself thinking about the months or minutes before the death and asking what you might have done. And accompanying these questions are often blaming and punishing thoughts such as

- I didn't do enough.
- I wasn't a good parent.
- I could've stopped it from happening.
- I wasn't there.
- I didn't listen.
- I didn't look.
- I am the reason for the death.
- I didn't take the time.
- I didn't ask.
- I didn't say what I was feeling.

— ❧ —

"We gather our arms full of guilt as though it were precious stuff.
It must be that we want it that way."[3]

John Steinbeck

— ❧ —

When you love, you become vulnerable. When you become vulnerable, you open yourself up to an array of emotions, and one of those may be guilt. Blaming yourself and others can be paralyzing, eventually weakening the process of moving forward. It can also lead to feelings of inadequacy, frustration, and depression. These are real feelings and emotions. To deny them is to pretend that all is well. Own these emotions, but take care that they don't own you. Let guilt be a motivator to move on in the process of healing.

Martha Whitmore Hickman, whose daughter died in a horse riding accident, said, "It is important, when dealing with all aspects of grief, to keep the process moving along. The temptation is to freeze, to stay perpetually recoiled against so terrible a blow."

— ⅔ —

"Guilt is not a response to anger; it is a response to one's own actions or lack of action. If it leads to change then it can be useful, since it is then no longer guilt but the beginning of knowledge."[4]

Audre Lorde, Sister Outsider: Essays and Speeches

— ⅔ —

To break the cycle of blame, it is sometimes helpful to honestly answer the two questions that are plaguing your thoughts:

1. If you had done something, what could have happened?

2. If you hadn't done that, what could have happened?

All of your answers will inevitably fall into two categories. Either you could have done more or you did all you could. But neither conclusion will bring your child back, and chances are you will never really know for sure if your actions or another person's actions would have made a difference. Allow yourself time to come to terms with these two conclusions.

FEELING RELIEF . . . WITH GUILT

There are elements of relief that may be apparent after the death of a child. This sounds crass and wrong. After all, you may think, *How could a parent possibly feel relief over the death of a child?* Nevertheless, it can happen.

Nikki: *A friend spent hours with her sick child at the hospital. She came to feel that the hospital was like a prison, and when her son died, she felt relief that she would never have to return to that institution. Afterward, she felt tremendous guilt because of that feeling of relief.*

Some parents deal with terminally ill children who are extremely depressed and fight their inner demons on a daily basis. Their medications may not work. Family life is in constant upheaval and uncertainty. Sleep is continually interrupted. Bills resulting from the problems faced by the child are hard to pay. There's little personal time for a parent in this situation. The child may be angry and unhappy. Many of these issues find resolution upon the death of the child.

Alice: *During Lora's medical treatments to try and cure her cancer, there were many trips to the Doernbecher Children's Hospital in Portland, Oregon (180 miles roundtrip). She also had two surgeries in Portland and one in*

Denver at the Children's Hospital. Though children heal quickly, it was not easy to see her wheeled into an operating room to be cut open once again. I spent many Tuesday and Thursday mornings at a pediatric office in a neighboring city, trying to calm Lora as they fed chemotherapy into her veins. It was painful physically for her, and this caused me to have a lot of emotional pain. Because her illness was prior to home computers and the Internet, Mark would spend hours away at the university library, trying to research potential cures for neuroblastoma. Trying to balance Lora's great medical needs with the needs of our five other children, ages four through twelve, was difficult also. There were many sleepless nights trying to ease Lora's belly pain, and watching her shrink from a lively, strong, normal toddler to a fourteen-pound twenty-month-old took its toll.

When she took her last breath, her pain was gone. My first reaction was calm and peaceful. We knew she was in a better place. I was also relieved that there would be no more surgeries, no more days away from my other children due to hospitalization, no more trying to coordinate Lora's health needs with the needs of five other active siblings, no more seeing Lora starve to death, and no more pain. With the relief came a sense of guilt. How could I feel relieved that my daughter died? What kind of parent ever felt that? It took years to realize that it was OK. These are emotions that come to the surface and cannot be denied. It's OK to desire a sense of peace. And yet, would I bring back the pain, the inconvenience, the surgeries, and so on for just one more day with her? My answer is always yes.

— ❦ —

"Guilt is perhaps the most painful companion of death."[5]

Elisabeth Kübler-Ross

— ❦ —

Nikki: There are emotions that I'm not proud of that surfaced during my early grieving stages. I felt an extreme guilt as Taylor's mother. I felt like I should have watched her more carefully. I felt self-pity to an extreme. I also found myself placing blame on others so that I wouldn't blame myself. These feelings never got me anywhere. There was no consistency in my emotions. Some days I wanted friends and family to talk about Taylor's death, and on other days I wanted everyone to pretend it didn't happen. I felt as though it was easier to act like nothing happened. I did not want to disrespect her, but sometimes it was *just easier to pretend life had always been this way. My guilt would eat away at me for this. The only way I found to combat these emotions was to forgive myself and focus on others. I feel like it's healthy to own up to these emotions and feelings and move on.*

Whether it be guilt or replaying the "what ifs" over and over again in your head, try to remember humanity comes with frailties and imperfections. We are all human. Learn to recognize how you feel after you go through the "what ifs" or the "I'm not a good parent" feelings. If this leaves you feeling inadequate, withdrawn, or depressed, seek for those thoughts that bring you peace. Concentrate on what will give you solace. If you feel guilt, begin the process of forgiving yourself.

THOUGHTS FROM OTHERS WHO HAVE LOST A CHILD

"Because I was the one there when Marc drowned, I dealt with guilt in addition to grief. I had never lost a loved one, and I never knew how bad it felt."

—Janet Harris, mother of Marc David Harris (1980–1986)

"When the negative emotions come, I try not to react in a harsh way or be too sensitive. I don't try to understand why things happen, and I just consider that they are for my experience and growth. Not only will they work out in my best interest, but someday I will understand."

—Karen Martin, mother of Lane Anthony Martin (1971-1982)

"I did the best I could. I made the best decisions with the information given at the time, and still the outcome was the same. He is gone. Now I have to rebuild me and give myself permission to cry when needed and enjoy the ups when they come."

—Shelley Merrill, mother of Cameron Merrill (2010–2013)

"Our son Scott was killed in July before his junior year at high school. When school started that fall, I found myself always looking for Scott whenever I was at school or driving by. Even a year later when Scott's brother, Greg, started his freshman year at the high school, I still found myself scanning a crowd of students to see if I could see Scott.

"One evening, I drove to the school to check with Greg about how he would be getting home after a basketball game. I scanned the student section looking for Greg and was able to locate him. After I got home, I realized that was the first time in a year and a half that I had been to the high school and had not found myself looking for Scott. The next week, I shared this experience with two of Scott's favorite teachers who were also my good friends. One of these dear teachers said to me, 'Don't feel guilty that you didn't look for Scott.' That was a moment of great healing for me."

—Diane Merten, mother of Scott Merten (1973–1990)

"My daughter died of SIDS while staying overnight with my mother. I received a phone call early in the morning telling me that there was a medical emergency with my baby and to go straight to the hospital. My husband was on his way to school, and I called him and told him to meet me there. He got there first. When they brought me into a waiting room, he told me through tears that she was gone. I threw myself to the ground and started thrashing around, unable to control my emotions or my body. When I had finally worn myself out and was forced to pause for breath, I was overcome with the thought that I had to believe that this would have happened anywhere. I refused to believe that if she had been somewhere else or if I had done something different that maybe she would still be alive. And every person I spoke to for the rest of that day I told that to. It would have happened anywhere. I did not want to burden my grief even more with blame or what ifs. I knew it would be a hard enough journey without adding more weight on my back."

—Candida Marie Knight, mother of Elena Marie Knight (2009–2010)

NOTES

1. Kris Carr, "How to Do Less and Live More," *Huffington Post*, accessed May 4, 2015, http://www.huffingtonpost.com/kris-carr/work-life-balance_b_2900848.html.
2. John O'Callaghan, Twitter, August 6, 2012 (9:36 a.m.), https://twitter.com/johnmaine/status/232515510011576320.
3. John Steinbeck, *East of Eden* (New York: Penguin, 2002), 267.
4. Audre Lorde, *Sister Outsider: Essays and Speeches* (Berkeley: Crossing Press, 2007), 130.
5. Elisabeth Kübler-Ross, *On Death and Dying* (New York: Macmillan, 1969).

6

TRIGGERS

"It is interesting how one word can spark memories that one believes she has buried beyond recognition."[1]

—Mandy Nachampassack-Maloney

THE SNEAKER WAVES OF GRIEF

Triggers cause response or reaction. Often, they take you by surprise when you're unprepared. In the grieving process, they are events, smells, songs, associations, and other things that remind you of the child you lost, and they heighten emotions when you least expect them. They may be positive affirmations that your child existed and played a crucial role in your life—that you loved him or her deeply and had a very special relationship. At the same time, they can be so painful, reminding you of your loss that you spin out of control.

C. S. Lewis wrote about the "waves of grief" in his book *A Grief Observed*, a memoir documenting the untimely death of his beloved wife. He likens grief to waves upon the beach. They can be massive amounts of seawater pounding the rocks and sand as they rise and hurl themselves on shore.

Sneaker waves can come from nowhere and can pull a bystander down into the tide when they least expect it. You may be having a day without sadness or heaviness. You're feeling happy and conversant, and you're moving forward. Then something triggers those waves of grief and you are smothered with emotions once again. You may be overcome with a whirlwind of depression, guilt, sadness, regret, or even an extreme awareness of what you have lost. It can be different every time you experience a trigger. One day a sock found behind the dryer can bring you to your knees with sorrow, and the next day it won't bother you at all.

Triggers are as varied as the sands of the sea. They may bring unexpected reminders of what you have lost. These triggers can even be memories that you thought were forgotten but are now in the forefront of your mind.

— ⸭ —

"Songs and smells will bring you back to a moment in
time more than anything else. It's amazing how much can be
conjured with a few notes of a song or a solitary whiff of a room.
A song you didn't even pay attention to at the time, a place
that you didn't even know had a particular smell."[2]

Emily Giffin

— ⸭ —

Alice: *Music is a trigger for me. Christopher Cross's song "Think of Laura" came out about the time of Lora's cancer diagnosis and death. The words spoke to me. I can't hear that song without tearing up. There is something unique about music. It has the ability to reach down into the inner parts of our soul. I remember going to church one day and feeling like my emotions were not going to get the best of me that day. I was in control. Then the congregation started to sing a hymn, and I had to get up and leave. There was something so beautiful about the music, the words, and the harmonies that triggered feelings of grief. After that experience, I tried to better prepare myself to be ready to feel those emotions.*

Here are some common triggers:

- words or melody of a song
- a holiday, birthday, or day that reminds you of your child
- smells associated with holidays, food, seasons, clothing, and people
- children who were the age of your child when he or she died
- any location that brings back memories of being with your child

- food enjoyed by your child
- learning of the death of a child who died in a similar manner
- people who were around when your child died
- weather or a time of year that signifies something relating to the death
- clothing that your child wore
- books that your child enjoyed
- high school graduation year if he or she died prior to that date
- their school work or drawing
- restaurants, movies, and parks he or she enjoyed
- pictures of the child
- places where your child slept, ate, played, or worked
- seeing your child's friends
- when your other children look or speak similar to the deceased child
- sound of the siren on an emergency vehicle
- learning of a new treatment or potential cure for the disease that took the life of your child
- world news or tragedies of any kind

SURFING THE WAVES

Each of us has our own triggers. Becoming familiar with the things that might bring recurring feelings of grief for you can help prepare you to handle certain situations calmly and rationally.

— ?❧ —

"Your mind can be either your prison or your palace.
What you make it is yours to decide."[3]

Bernard Kelvin Clive

— ?❧ —

When a trigger strikes, what we do depends on what we want to feel. There are times when we want to remember. We want to be able to listen to a song that has deep meaning and memories for us. We may want to open a box of special items that belonged to our child and hold each item as we cherish and relish the memories. Or perhaps you want to be with your child's friends and hear them recall shared experiences. It's OK to initiate or linger through a trigger. Remembering is good—it's how your loved one lives on.

Then there are other times when you don't want to handle the weight of the memories. Perhaps you are simply emotionally exhausted and know that a memory or trigger will force you into a dark place that you just can't go.

Become familiar with the triggers that play havoc with your emotions. Most of us have lost only one child. We are amateurs at this game. It's like being a parent for the first time. Where was the practice course? No one gave us that foolproof parent manual. So it is with the loss of a child. You are thrown into a terrifying situation, without any prior experience. With time, you will gain that experience and know how to handle the triggers.

TRY THIS
Dark places need to be replaced with light. Think of a happy moment with your child. Remember a time in your life when you experienced joy. You may need to replace the darkness with a completely unconnected experience. Maybe you need to take a walk, turn on the TV, call someone, read a magazine, or say a prayer.

— ❦ —

I am not afraid of storms, for I am learning how to sail my ship.[4]

Louisa May Alcott

— ❦ —

Emotions are blurred when grief is fresh, and at these times, we may not know what is best for ourselves. Don't ignore the triggers, but learn from them. Think of a surfer. Initially, he or she will watch the swells, gauge the size of the waves, and learn where the wave will break that day. A surfer rides a wave and isn't sucked under but maneuvers just in front of the crest of the wave.

Be ready. When your emotions are triggered, the wave hits. Your first waves will be the hardest. Try to ride the crest of the wave into shore.

THOUGHTS FROM OTHERS WHO HAVE LOST A CHILD

"It is amazing to me that, even after so many years, there are still triggers that grip me. I generally remove myself from trigger situations and become quiet, responding with silence. I recall something I have memorized and repeat it in my mind, or I reward myself with something to eat, read, or do after such an episode."

—Karen Martin, mother of Lane Anthony Martin (1971–1982)

"Birthdays are the hardest for me. When I gave birth to baby Elena, I could never have imagined how great a journey of growing, grieving, and then healing her spirit would take me on. And even though her birthdays don't give me the chance to see how she's grown, I take the day to cherish her and see how she's helped me to grow."

—Candida Marie Knight, mother of Elena Marie Knight (2009–2010)

"A trigger can be someone saying something about his or her family or Christmas celebrations or being at a place or event that brings back memories. In an attempt to handle these emotions, I try to change what I am thinking about or avoid places and events that bring back memories. We are still freshly dealing with grief, and I realize that I can't use avoidance long term."

—Beth Nelson, mother of Joshua Roland Nelson (1992–2012)

"With Lindsay, it is the time of year on the calendar that triggers emotional feelings for me. She was born on January 24 and died two weeks later from complications of pneumonia. I noticed that I was always more emotional during that time of the year. I just warn people now that I may have a hard time in January and early February. With Lynette, our daughter who died shortly before her thirtieth birthday of alcohol poisoning, the triggers take the form of songs, pictures, family videos, sunflowers, seeing something she would have liked, and watching her friends settle down and have children. That last one can be a tough trigger too."

—Shanna Miller, mother of Lindsay Miller (1978–1978)
and Lynette Miller (1981–2011)

"When I see a cyclist or a runner or someone walking toward me in the forest near our home, I just crumble inside . . . wanting him, longing to see him. And when I hear a helicopter, it can literally bring me to my knees as I reflect on him being taken off of the mountain. I am trying to change these images and turn them into gratitude. I know in time I will. For now, I just let the feeling wash into me. There is no other way."

—*Pat Newport, mother of Alex Newport-Berra, 1981–2014*

"The triggers for me are still the sounds of emergency response sirens. When I first hear them, it makes me feel sick. I try to remind myself that those sounds mean help is on the way."

—*Brenda Kingsley, mother of Hannah Marie Kingsley (2004–2009)*

"Life can be a trigger. Every day, years after Dustin's death, I never know when something will trigger grief. It could be watching a family interacting with one another. It can be an emotional song. It can be a memory that surfaces."

—*Debora Eichelberger, mother of Dustin Guy Eichelberger (1985–2000)*

"One of my students came into the office for the first time. He stood at my desk. I swear he had the same hands and body structure as my Jas. All I wanted was to walk around my desk and cry and hug him and hold his hands in mine. I think I would've been fired! There are so many triggers, but I try to keep things compartmentalized. There's a time and a place for my true grieving."

—*Gina Newcomb, mother of Jas Newcomb (1980–2005)*

"There are too many triggers to list. At first I couldn't handle them. Then I named it the 'tornado of pain.' My therapist told me to picture myself growing roots to anchor myself to the ground so I wasn't caught up in the swirl of pain and hurt. Then I could mentally look up and pick out which hurt to spend time with and get through. She also told me to see my grief as a wave. You can fight the wave, but it will still come and knock you down. Or you can anticipate the wave, ride it out, mentally observe it, and go with it. You know all the while that the wave will recede at some point and give you a break from the pain but that another wave is coming—it's just a matter of time. I learn from this experience by observing, not judging or telling myself how I *should* feel."

—*Shelley Merrill, mother of Cameron Merrill (2010–2013)*

"The main trigger for me is seeing newborn babies. Unstoppable grief and wicked jealousy bubbles within me when I see a newborn baby."

—*Caitlin Bradshaw, mother of Emma Joy Bradshaw (2013–2013)*

"My trigger is being in town and seeing a little blonde girl about Hannah's age with her back to me and having that split-second thought that it is her, and then realizing it's not. But everything is a trigger: a picture, a commercial on TV, and little Easter dresses on sale in the spring and costumes for little girls at Halloween. Some are like a kick in the chest. Sometimes I can ignore them and walk on. Most of the time, I feel good and use that trigger to have a good thought about Hannah. Her picture is in every room in my house, and I like that. Good or bad, I don't want to forget Hannah."

—*Gary Kingsley, father of Hannah Marie Kingsley (2004–2009)*

NOTES

1. Mandy Nachampassack-Maloney, *Asha in Time* (Los Gatos: Smashwords, 2010), 244.
2. Emily Giffin, *Something Borrowed* (New York: St. Martin's Paperbacks, 2004),
3. Bernard Kelvin Clive, *Your Dreams Will Not Die* (Accra: Dreametrix, 2010).
4. Louisa May Alcott, *Little Women* (New York: Grosset & Dunlap, 1947), 596.

7

HEALTHY HEALING

*"And once the storm is over you won't remember how you made
it through, how you managed to survive. You won't even be sure,
in fact, whether the storm is really over. But one thing is certain.
When you come out of the storm you won't be the same person who
walked in. That's what the storm is all about."*[1]

—Haruki Murakami

REGAINING HAPPINESS AND STRENGTH

"Will I ever be happy again?" In the midst of loss, this question is inevitable. You may not feel it is possible at this time, but the simple answer is yes. Every human has the capacity to heal. If you break a bone in your arm, the body has the capacity to heal itself. New bone mass will grow, but a proper setting of the bone at the time of break is important. The bone will never heal exactly as it was before, but it can heal to work just as properly and efficiently as prior to the fracture. In fact, a broken bone that has healed is often stronger than the original. Similarly, your heart has the capacity to heal from grief. In fact, you may even come to know a personal strength that you had not known previously, but facing your pain with a healthy mind-set is crucial to the process.

We have all heard that time is a great healer. But during the minutes, hours, and days immediately following death, this is hard to imagine. Time stands still and becomes irrelevant. You are numb, days blur, and there is no healing balm as time passes. But it can happen, even if ever so slowly—day by day, month by month, and then year by year. As those days and years pass, they are replaced with perspective and experiences. The warm knife in your heart can be pulled out slowly, leaving a wound to be healed over time. The damaged tissue turns pink again, and the scar, though it remains, becomes smoother and less noticeable. The heart can still ache and feel pain, but not so brutally.

— ❧ —

"The difference between stumbling blocks and stepping-stones is how you use them."

Unknown

— ❧ —

WAYS TO HEAL

Grief is not a mental illness but rather a process in which there's lots of room to heal at your own pace. There is no overnight fix, but with time you'll grow to deal with your grief and pain in rational, healthy ways. Some of these methods to help in the healing process may be therapy, support groups, healthy outlets, or medication.

Therapy

Many grieving parents may want to seek out professional counseling from a trained therapist. Getting professional help does not mean you are weak or helpless. It doesn't make you or define you, but rather it provides someone with whom to share your thoughts. This person is trained to recognize feelings and can help you understand what is happening inside your head and heart. Therapy will often provide tools to help you in the grieving process, and the sooner you receive access to those tools, the better.

Alice: *Mark and I had heard stories of how common divorce was among couples who had lost a child. Even though our relationship was strong, we felt it was important to have a counselor help us work through some of the issues of guilt and blame that compounded with Lora's death. The counseling sessions made a big difference. We were able to express our fears and thoughts in a safe, neutral environment and feel that we were both heard and understood. Relationships can be strained after the death of a child. The image of two people coming together in support and love because they have lost a child is not always accurate. Loss is stressful. It does things with your mind and heart.*

You may question yourself and your belief system. You may be tempted to place blame. Anticipate that you may need individual, couple, or family counseling. Find names of counselors who trusted people have recommended. And if you don't feel a "fit" with your first counselor, choose another.

Support Groups

Find support of one type or another. It may be family, friends, spiritual leaders, support groups, counselors, or medical professionals. Perhaps you just need someone to listen to you and validate your feelings and insecurities. Let yourself be vulnerable and seek the help you need. Don't try to work through your grief alone.

Grief support groups can be helpful. At these support groups, you realize that you are not alone in grief—that many others are struggling with similar issues. This setting allows individuals to feel acknowledged as they open up about their deepest pain in a safe, nonjudgmental atmosphere.

Laurie Russell of Benton Hospice in Corvallis, Oregon, shares, "You can also find grief support by reaching out to your local hospice. Most nonprofit hospices offer grief support to the family whether or not the child was under hospice care."

Healthy Outlets

We are all afraid of becoming overwhelmed. As you take care of yourself, you may need some help—someone or something to serve as your outlet. This outlet may be an activity like exercise, shopping, meditation, or journaling.

Find what helps you heal. Is it talking with friends? Is it joining a sports team? Is it reading books? Is it writing a blog or communicating on social media? Perhaps it would help to take a class and develop a new skill like tennis, photography, pottery, or speaking in another language. Learn something you didn't know before.

TRY THIS
Every morning, start your day with a short pep talk. Write affirming words on a note and put it on your mirror or write it down to carry in your purse or wallet. Say something like, "I am a strong person—stronger than I know," "I can make it through this day," or "I can choose to be happy."

Alice: *About four months after Lora died, Mark and I decided we needed to do something together to build our relationship and have fun. So we took a swing dance class. It was great therapy and something we enjoyed. It gave us something else to focus on besides our grief. We also felt joy because we were both developing a skill. We never became experts in the "swing," but we felt we had learned the basics and had a good time in the process.*

Nikki: *Find your outlet and set up time to make it happen. My outlet was writing down my feelings. I tried to get my husband to do the same. After many conversations about this, he finally wrote in his journal, but it wasn't helpful for him. What seemed to help was golfing, a sport that allowed him to work out his frustrations and be outside. He could commune with God as he was out on the course and always came back with a happier disposition. For me, writing my frustrations on a piece of paper made all the difference in my emotional stability. Here is an embarrassing rant that I wrote late one night, about three months after Taylor died, when grief struck so hard I wanted to scream:*

> *I don't understand why everyone says the wrong thing. I feel like my husband is so insensitive because he doesn't see the death date as a day that will mean he misses her more than the next. Now, while I know this is not logical, I still have a hard time with it. I wake up every day and miss my daughter. I carried her for nine months and helped her develop into the beautiful girl she was. I can't just stop caring about her. I can't stop thinking about her every moment when each day before the accident I spent my days caring for her every need. It makes me ache that she's not part of our daily activities. I see the people around me busy in their mundane lives and I think, How can you worry about all the little things that don't matter when I've lost a child? Does that make them insensitive? No. It just means people aren't obsessed with your problems like you are. People are consumed by what they knew, what they know now, and what will affect their futures. I'm starting to feel like she's fading into the background and no one will remember her. I HATE THAT. She is still part of my daily routine. Now it's just a mental routine. I get sick of being strong, the one people look up to, and the mom with all the answers. I'm tired. I feel wiped out and I haven't done anything physical. Sleep is an escape. I love to sleep off the hurt. No one wants to talk about it anymore, and I'm not sure how I feel about this.*

Once I wrote down these thoughts and feelings, I felt better. For some reason I felt like I was heard and understood. Even though my words were just on paper, they were out of me and that was exhilarating.

Medication

Grieving is a process that requires the brain to learn new things. The trauma associated with the death of a child is profound and can have emotional, psychological, and physical effects. Each person will react differently to this situation, so there is no medical advice or prescription that fits all.

Some have concluded that taking medication at a time of loss can be an escape and, therefore, should be avoided. For others, it may be the only way to make it through the crisis. Having a good night's sleep following the death of a child can make a difference in how you approach the decisions and tasks that accompany this loss. In extreme cases, medication can also be life-saving if severe depression is apparent.

Being heavily sedated or "tranquilized" as you walk through the difficult steps of grief may not be the best solution. Spending quality time in conversation with supportive family members, friends, or counselors will prove to be a better long-term solution toward making real progress in the grief process.

This is a time to consult with your physician, counselor, or other professional. Let them know what you are experiencing, and work together on the decision to use medication or not. When medication is needed, the two most common classes of drugs used to help with grief are antidepressants and anxiolytics (tranquilizers).

1. Antidepressants

Depression, for some, is a chronic mental state, and for others will only occur at times of severe and persistent stress, such as occurs when a loved one dies. In depression, there are actual changes in the level of chemicals in the brain that are responsible for proper function. You might think of it in this way: A large part of your brain, the frontal lobes, functions to allow you to feel optimistic, be creative, love, solve problems, and experience joy. If that area of the brain has a lowered level of the chemicals that allow one nerve to connect with another (we have millions of these), then the result will be gloom, a lack of joy, and feeling like you cannot go on. This is depression. Medications that treat depression can raise these neurotransmitter chemicals and literally bring back some hope and the expectation that joy will return. For people who have pre-existing depression, grieving can make the condition worse, and antidepressant medications may also be helpful at these times.

2. Anxiolytics

Anxiety, when it spirals out of control, can be a terrifying experience. We are all wired differently and will therefore experience different body reactions to the worst news of our lives. For one, there may be rage, anger, and even open hysteria, while another might seek solitude and weep alone. Headaches may be intense, nausea and abdominal pain may occur and last for days, or an individual may experience a racing heart or feel like they are suffocating. Others may put on a happy face and appear to be in control, while actually feeling a deep sense of terror or fear. When in the midst of grieving, you may have a strong yearning for some relief from the agony, even if it is just for a short time. Avoid excessive use of alcohol, and be cautious about taking benzodiazepines (tranquilizers) because they can impair your ability to make proper decisions or drive safely and can be addictive. But under the guidance of your treating clinician, these medications may be beneficial so that your severe anxiety or sleeplessness can fade to relaxation or desperately needed sleep.

AVOID NEGATIVE ESCAPE ROUTES

Though medical and psychology research on grief may differ, most professionals agree that there are negative ways to deal with grief. These may include the following:

- misuse of alcohol or other drugs
- self-inflicted harm
- total denial
- suicidal thoughts or attempts
- causing pain or harm to others

When any of these methods take hold of your life, we urge you to seek professional help.

Nikki: *As I grew up, I was never tempted by alcohol or anything else that altered the senses. I had been taught that these things weren't good for our bodies. Even in high school, alcohol was never a temptation, although its consumption seemed to make you "part of the in crowd." But I would be lying if the thought of alcohol didn't enter my mind after Taylor's death. I wanted so badly to "not feel" anything. I wanted to numb out the pain. I knew deep down that this was not the answer. Instead, I took one minute, one hour, and one day at a time until I could accept in a healthy way the emotions that came. It can be done.*

— ❧ —

"You gain strength, courage, and confidence by every experience in
which you really stop to look fear in the face. . . .
You must do the thing which you think you cannot do."[2]

Eleanor Roosevelt

— ❧ —

Healthy healing can happen. There may not be a specific timetable,
and you may need the help of professionals to provide you with tools and
information. But choosing to heal is the foundation of healthy healing.
Millions have chosen to heal. You can make that choice also.

THOUGHTS FROM OTHERS WHO HAVE LOST A CHILD

"If needed, get a prescription from a qualified therapist. It helps, but
you still have to work through your emotions. Someone told me it was
OK to yell and scream to help let the pain out. I did this only privately, in
our car, when no one was around."

—*Janet Harris, mother of Marc David Harris (1980–1986)*

"Talking to others helped me with the healing process. I had a counselor come from Hospice for about six visits, and that helped a lot because
I still needed to talk but other people in my life had heard it all from me."

—*Susan Fisher, mother of Dallan Fisher (1988–1992)*

"I read many books on death and bereavement. I went to four different
counselors and attended a support group for parents who had lost children called Compassionate Friends. I think all of these processes helped,
but it is difficult when you never anticipated that your child would pre-
cede you in death. No one else can work through bereavement for you.
You just have to work through it on your own."

—*Karen Martin, mother of Lane Anthony Martin (1971–1982)*

"I read and listen to novels as a distraction; they give me a break from
the pain. I talk about Sam to people who are emotionally safe. They don't
try to fix it, they don't offer platitudes, and they let me be where I am
emotionally and are not uncomfortable when I cry. I talk to a counselor
once a month. I have a little retreat house at the coast where I can go and

get away from everyday life. I go there to physically and emotionally rest."

—*Ann Lahr, mother of Sam Lahr (1989–2009)*

"We were inundated with books on grieving. I did read through some of them and found some things to be helpful. I went to counseling briefly but found other things to be more helpful. These things included writing down Hannah's favorite things—her songs, books, colors, foods, and so on. I didn't want to forget these things, and I wanted to be able to share this with Hannah's younger brother so he could know a little of whom she was. Also, writing down memories of the journey God had taken us on was a reminder that He was there through it all and would continue to be."

—*Brenda Kingsley, mother of Hannah Marie Kingsley (2004–2009)*

"Keeping busy helped me when our first child, Lindsay, died at only two weeks old. I also found a huge amount of comfort serving others. One friend who had her baby during the time that Lindsay was in the hospital would let me "borrow" her baby sometimes as I ached to hold a baby. I read everything I could get my hands on—books by people who shared near death experiences and books and articles regarding death and dying. It was vastly different when Lynette, our adult child died over thirty years later. As Lindsay was our first child, there were no siblings at her death to think about. With Lynette's death from alcohol poisoning, her three surviving siblings, as well as a nephew (our grandson) who knew and loved Lynette, were traumatized as well. That was a huge concern to me as a parent and grandparent. The things that helped me with Lynette were reading additional books on grief, having friends who let me talk, going through Lynette's things and 'figuring out' what happened. We also found support through the Hospice organization. I initially thought of Hospice only for end of life, as in those with long-term illnesses, cancer, and so on. This is not true. All of their bereavement services were offered at no cost. One of the best resources was a monthly newsletter from Hospice."

—*Shanna Miller, mother of Lindsay Miller (1978–1978)*
and Lynette Miller (1981–2011)

"It helps me to know that talking about and remembering Dustin is not 'off-limits.' These memories may be hard to think about, but they are not harmful."

—*Debora Eichelberger, mother of Dustin Guy Eichelberger (1985–2000)*

"I write poetry to help with the grieving process. I also talk to my husband and daughter and Jas's best friend, Chris, about the good and bad. We laugh about his sense of humor, and we cry about the missing part of our little family."

—*Gina Newcomb, mother of Jas Newcomb (1980–2005)*

"I enjoy talking about Troy. He often comes up in conversations with family and friends. Sometimes I get a little teary, but mostly it feels good to celebrate his life in this way. One day, I was talking to my fourteen-year-old grandson, Logan. His dad, Dennis, died a year and a half before his uncle, Troy. Dennis and Troy were good friends. We were talking about how difficult it is to believe they are really gone. We keep expecting them to walk in the door or call us. He said something that touched my heart: 'You know, Grandma, I've been at this longer than you have, and you don't forget, but it does get easier.' What a wise young man."

—*Judy Juntunen, mother of Troy Juntunen (1967–2012)*

"Keeping busy with five other little kids was a comfort to me. I talked to my mom a lot. Megan's death was unexpected, but I felt gratitude and mercy throughout the grieving process. Life had been hard for Megan. I felt a sense of freedom that she was no longer burdened with this life. I seemed to skip over the anger stage. Death was not unknown to me, as I had already lost a sister and three grandparents."

—*Elaine Forrest, mother of Megan Forrest (1985–2005)*

"Having lost all my older relatives and nearly all my closest friends, I have had a lot of grief experience, and I continue to contain my anger and frustration with the grim process of aging and dying that we all have to endure. Our son handled his own behavior in a courageous, loving way, trying to make things as easy as possible for us family members. I realized this and complimented him for it. He replied that he was doing the best he could do to make things easy for us. His example probably helped me to cope more than anything else did."

—*Craig Leman, father of Craig A. Leman (1956–1998)*

"The grieving process is different for each one of us. I don't know your child, and I don't know you. I can empathize, but I really don't know how it is affecting you. Only you know. And that's OK. Don't do it alone. You owe it to those around you to get help. You may have other children or a spouse who is grieving. To help them, you need to help yourself. Talk with friends, a pastor, or a counselor. There is nothing wrong with going to counseling. There is something wrong with pretending you can go through it alone. It will be five years since Hannah died in 2009. I still see a counselor; I go once a week for four to five months and then I take a six-month break. Counseling is hard, but it helps. A counselor once told me that you can go to counseling or you can have a nervous breakdown. Sometimes, there's no in-between. I think that has been true for me. I wouldn't have made it without the counseling. Today I feel good and I have been good for quite a while. The pain is still close by. Not as sharp as it used to be, but still hard. I don't want to be over Hannah. I am happy where I am now."

—*Gary Kingsley, father of Hannah Marie Kingsley (2004–2009)*

"To help with the grieving process, I would write on my blog. Having to sit, ponder, and put words to my feelings gave them a more solid shape. I could more easily understand and process my emotions, and after each entry I felt an immediate release. Though showcasing my feelings so publicly did come at a cost. While so many of my readers gave me strength and support, I did have several people who had negative responses to my grieving process. As raw as my loss was, this was really hard for me and damaged some of the healing headway I had made. So my advice is to know yourself and your audience before opening yourself up completely."

—*Candida Marie Knight, mother of Elena Marie Knight (2009–2010)*

"Someone said to me, early on, 'There's nothing like the death of a child to rearrange your address book.' How true. One of biggest things for me was the friends who did show up . . . and those who didn't. Some close friends who I assumed would be there, would know what to say, what to do . . . disappeared. And some who I didn't see as often were there (and still are after many months) 'in spades.' It was grief upon grief for me to not hear from some people. I would lay awake nights, making up stories for them as to why they weren't in touch. Now, I spend time feeling grateful for the friends who *are* there."

—*Pat Newport, mother of Alex Newport-Berra (1981–2014)*

"Alice and I found profound words of support while reading books together. Works by Rabbi Harold Kushner, C. S. Lewis, and Elisabeth Kübler-Ross were especially beneficial and helped us know we were not alone in the world of grieving."

—*Mark Rampton, father of Lora Dorothea Rampton (1984–1986)*

"We had a great support team after Cameron's death. Dr. Aaron David, our family doctor, was our first line of defense and helped us with medications and setting the support team. Next in our line of defense was our family therapist, Katy Trautman. The last important part of this team was developing a relationship with a bereavement community that helped in the 'no one knows what this feels like' period. Candlelighters for Children with Cancer offered important advice and a wonderful bereavement program. Our local Benton County Hospice provided an excellent grief program that was for anyone, not just those using hospice for end-of-life needs. Their Camp Compass was super helpful for my other children. This diverse team, made up of different individuals and organizations, gave us the appropriate tools to face grief from every angle."

—*Shelley and Cressey Merrill, parents of Cameron Merrill (2010–2013)*

NOTES

1. Haruki Murakami, *Kafka on the Shore* (New York: Random House, 2005), 5–
2. Eleanor Roosevelt, quoted in *Gutsy Women: More Travel Tips and Wisdom for the Road by Marybeth Bond* (San Francisco: Travelers' Tales, 2001).

8

WELL-MEANING COMMENTS AND QUESTIONS

"My child died. I don't need advice. All I need is for you to gently close your mouth, open wide your heart, and walk with me until I can see in color again."[1]

—Angela Miller

GOOD INTENTIONS, POOR DELIVERY

For many, death is an uncomfortable subject. People can make sense of a ninety-five-year-old woman who lived a good life and peacefully died in her sleep. They can't make sense of someone young dying "before their time." Friends and family members will try to reason this out in their own minds, and they will grieve too. But their grief will be different than yours. Consequently, their comments, which are intended to help and offer support, may be painful.

Here are some actual comments and questions that the parents who have contributed to this book received after losing their child. You may hear similar comments. We have added possible thoughts that a grieving parent may think in response.

- "Your child is in a better place."
  (What was so bad about the loving home I created for my child?)

- "Other people have it worse than you."
  (What could be worse than the pain I am feeling?)

- "I can sort of understand; my cat died last year."

(A loving relationship with a pet can be deep and meaningful, but that is different than the relationship between me and my child.)

- "Everything happens for a reason."
(What logical "reason" could there be for any child's death?)

- "With him being so ill, I'm sure you knew he would die soon."
(No, I held onto hope for a cure.)

- "How did your child die?"
(I will give you the benefit of the doubt that you have a genuine interest in my child. I hope that your question is not just morbid curiosity.)

- "I know just how you feel."
(Nobody knows how I feel. Your circumstances may be similar, but the relationship I had with my child was unique.)

- "Are you over it yet?"
(I don't think I will ever be "over it.")

- "Are you done grieving?"
(The loss of a child is never "done.")

- "At least you have other children."
(No one can replace my child who has died. The pain is not less because I have other children.)

- "You have a belief in God so you'll be OK."
(I do believe in God, but I'm not "OK." Sometimes I wonder why a loving God would allow this to happen.)

- "She would have suffered if she had lived."
(Logic is hollow right now. There are children who survived a similar accident, disease, or suicide attempt and are doing just fine.)

- "Make lemonade out of lemons."
(You can't compare my child's life to lemons and lemonade. It's not that easy for me to spin this tragedy instantly into some kind of a positive event.)

- "Can you have more children?"
(That is personal and none of your business.)

- "It could be worse."

(How do you know? I can't imagine anything worse than what has happened to my family.)

- "This is a test."
(And what happens if I flunk? Why isn't the test given to everyone?)

- "You lost one child. Imagine how hard it must be when entire families die in a holocaust or natural disaster."
(I can't imagine this horror, but should I feel joyous that it was only one person: my child?)

- "At least your child was just a baby."
(The age doesn't matter. My child died.)

- "At least your child had the chance to grow and experience life."
(The age doesn't matter. My child died.)

WHAT'S *NOT* SAID

Although many comments may be hurtful and even angering, sometimes a lack of comments can be worse. You may encounter conversations with people who know your child has died but who awkwardly don't mention it; this can feel as though your child never even existed. Chances are, the person you're talking to is simply too uncomfortable to bring it up or fears saying something wrong.

Yet you may appreciate someone simply saying, "I'm sorry to hear about your loss." This gives you the invitation to share more with them if you wish or just end the conversation with a thank you.

— ❧ —

"Remember not only to say the right thing in the
right place, but far more difficult still, to leave unsaid
the wrong thing at the tempting moment."[2]

Benjamin Franklin

— ❧ —

Nikki: *I've had people ignore me because they want to avoid such an uncomfortable topic. It was hurtful when, for months after we lost our daughter, I saw acquaintances literally walk the other direction when they saw me from a distance. I understand that it's uncomfortable, but that hurt worse than* *having them say "the wrong thing" to me. I always preferred being asked, "How are you dealing with things today?" instead of "How are you doing today?" It's so common to start a conversation with this second question that it doesn't really express a genuine interest.*

Most people don't intend to cause pain when they ask hurtful questions. Nor do they mean harm when they avoid saying anything. Remember that they likely feel uncomfortable and simply don't know what to say. Give them some slack. Before the deaths of our children, we might have done the same thing.

> **TRY THIS**
> When someone makes an inappropriate comment or asks a hurtful question, take a deep breath and simply say, "Thank you for sharing" or "The pain from losing a child can be unbearable." Most often they haven't been there and they just don't get it.

THE DREADED QUESTION

How many children do you have?

You will hear this question throughout the rest of your life. After the death of your child, there is uncertainty on how to reply. What do you say? Do you include your child who has died in the number? If you don't include them, are you forgetting them? Does everyone who asks this question really want to hear the whole story?

Alice: *It depends on who I am talking to and the depth of our relationship when answering this question. In more superficial relationships, I can reply, "We raised six children." With someone I trust, I usually phrase the comment with, "We have seven children, and one died when she was a child."*

Nikki: *There are several ways to answer truthfully without giving too much information. For me, it depends on the situation. If it is a short encounter with a stranger and I am just making conversation, I will usually say, "I have three children with me." If it is someone I feel comfortable with, I may say, "I'm currently raising three. I had a daughter pass away at sixteen months." If my children are within earshot of the question, then I always say, "I have four children but one passed away." This way, my kids realize that their little sister will always be a part of us. Sometimes I will say, "I have a nine-year-old boy, seven-year-old girl, and four-year-old girl." I will then make the choice to elaborate or not.*

Here are some additional perspectives from parents who have lost a child on how you can tackle this question and feel confident about what you share:

"I really struggled with how to answer this question. There was a risk of being asked their ages, and then what would I say? Did I really want to explain? Sometimes I answered four and other times five. With the passing of time, I now answer five. Hannah still is my child and still part of my life. I realize there really isn't a right or wrong answer; I just need to answer with what works for me."

—Brenda Kingsley, mother of Hannah Marie Kingsley (2004–2009)

"I am the mother of five children, but two of them have died. So when someone asks me about how many children I have, sometimes I'll explain that I'm the mother of five children and three of them are living." If people want to follow-up, they can. Other times, I'll say I have three children."

—Shanna Miller, mother of Lindsay Miller (1978–1978)
and Lynette Miller (1981–2011)

"We usually answer with, 'Five, ranging in age from ten to twenty-two.' If they ask more detail about each child, we will say that one died."

—Beth Nelson, mother of Joshua Roland Nelson (1992–2012)

"Mostly I have been asked, 'Do you have children?' I would then say I have a son who goes to Oregon State University and talk about him a bit and the conversation goes on. Only recently have I been asked if I have other children. In that case, I said I had another son who we lost a few years ago. My counselor told me that I get to decide who gets access. This has been a good tool for me when a question comes up about Sam. ("How did he die?") If I'm not comfortable having that discussion with the person asking the question, I say that I really can't or don't want to talk about it."

—Ann Lahr, mother of Sam Lahr (1989–2009)

"I have six children! I had six children on July 7, 2000, and I still have six children. I am not uncomfortable telling people I have six children."

—Debora Eichelberger, mother of Dustin Guy Eichelberger (1985–2000)

"I used to reply with the answer 'two sons,' but then they would follow up with the question, 'What are their ages?' I finally rationalized that Lane would understand that it wasn't that I didn't love him or want to acknowledge his life, but answering 'one son' would allow me to avoid the pain."

—*Karen Martin, mother of Lane Anthony Martin (1971–1982)*

"We simply say, 'We have eight children. Seven are living.'"

—*Janet Harris, mother of Marc David Harris (1980–1986)*

There will be situations that don't warrant going into a lengthy explanation about the death of your child. In other cases, you may feel safe and trust someone enough to open up your vulnerability to them. There isn't a right or wrong answer. Find the ones that work for you.

THOUGHTS FROM OTHERS WHO HAVE LOST A CHILD

"It was usually the people who did more listening than talking that helped me. The fewer the words used to express their condolences seemed to heal the most. The comment that still heals my heart came from a family friend. We had been visiting at her house, and after a while, she simply reached over and put her hand on my shoulder and said, 'I am so sorry about your baby.' I told her thanks and that everyone has something. And her response was simply, 'But that is a pretty big something.' This seven-word statement completely acknowledged my trial. So many people tried to shake me out of my grief by telling me how other people have it worse. One person mentioned that victims of the Holocaust lost not just their babies but also their entire families. I was in the most raw and exposed state of mind and could not understand why people felt that telling me about situations they found to be worse than mine would help."

—*Candida Marie Knight, mother of Elena Marie Knight (2009–2010)*

"After Emma died we were told some well-meaning things that stung because we were experiencing such fresh grief. For example when someone would say, 'She's in a better place,' I would think, *No, she should be with her mother.* When the comment was made, 'This is what was supposed to happen,' I would think, *Not true. Babies aren't supposed to die.* Another hurtful comment was, 'The pain will lessen with time.' When I first heard this, it was not what I wanted to hear. At that moment, I wanted to feel her loss. If I didn't feel pain, would that mean that I was OK with her loss? Although it is true that the pain lessens with time, these comments were not helpful to me. As time passed, these things didn't bother me as much."

—Caitlin Bradshaw, mother of Emma Joy Bradshaw
(August 14, 2013–August 15, 2013)

"I was irritated beyond words by well-intentioned religious people who said Craig's death was God's will when it was a profound, evil, tragic freak of nature."

—Craig Leman, father of Craig A. Leman (1956–1998)

"The most helpful thing people said was that they were praying for our family and they loved us. It doesn't seem like much, but it is enough. What else can you really say? The most painful comments from people were that she is in a better place, that the pain will pass, and that we need to look for the good. Yes, she is in a better place, but that doesn't change my pain. I rejoice that she is in God's presence, but I still hurt like hell. Hannah was pure sunlight, and I will never feel her warmth again in this lifetime. The pain doesn't pass. It has been five years, and as I sit and type this, I feel a dagger ripping through my chest. Don't try to understand. Pray for me, cry for me, show some love for my family, but most of all, just be quiet."

—Gary Kingsley, father of Hannah Marie Kingsley (2004–2009)

NOTES

1. Angela Miller, "6 Things to Never Say to a Bereaved Parent," *Still Standing Magazine*, accessed May 4, 2015, http://stillstandingmag.com/2014/01/6-things-never-say-bereaved-parent/.

2. Benjamin Franklin, quoted in L. L. Owens *Benjamin Franklin: The Inventive Founding Father* (Edina: ABDO Publishing Company, 2008), 101.

9

RELATIONSHIPS UNDER STRESS—SPOUSE OR SIGNIFICANT OTHER

"Death ends a life, not a relationship."[1]

—Mitch Albom

Khalil Gibran expressed relationships this way,

> Let there be spaces in your togetherness, And let the winds of the heavens dance between you. Love one another but make not a bond of love: Let it rather be a moving sea between the shores of your souls. Fill each other's cup but drink not from one cup. Give one another of your bread but eat not from the same loaf. Sing and dance together and be joyous, but let each one of you be alone, even as the strings of a lute are alone though they quiver with the same music. Give your hearts, but not into each other's keeping. For only the hand of Life can contain your hearts. And stand together, yet not too near together: For the pillars of the temple stand apart, and the oak tree and the cypress grow not in each other's shadow.[2]

DEATH'S IMPACT ON A RELATIONSHIP

At the time of birth, most parents experience great hopes and expectations for their newborn. These dreams can be shattered when a child dies. Although individuals will deeply grieve the loss of their child, grieving together through this loss usually comes with many unexpected obstacles and challenges. Any relationship, healthy or otherwise, will be affected by the loss of a child. If a marriage or a relationship is struggling before the death of a child, this loss will likely not strengthen the union. That does not mean that the relationship is doomed, but it does mean that it may take longer to restore that marriage or relationship to a situation with healthier communication than was previously experienced.

Families come in all sizes and situations. Given the prevalence of couples divorcing or separating, children today live in a variety of circumstances and family settings. If the parents of a child have divorced and remarried, the result can be several individuals struggling with the loss instead of just two. Stepparents can be very involved in the lives of their children. In addition, many children are born to a single parent today. There are some children who enter this world through anonymous in vitro fertilization. Parents can suffer as two individuals under the same roof or miles apart. No matter where they are or their family configuration, parents will experience differing degrees of challenge, loss, stress, and impact.

Dr. Sean Brotherson, associate professor and extension family life specialist at North Dakota University, has studied the effects of the loss of a child on marital and partner relationships. Brotherson has also written a book entitled *Parental Accounts of a Child's Death: Influences on Parental Identity and Behavior*. Although many studies have suggested that the divorce rate is higher among couples who have lost a child, Brotherson believes these studies are limited and, in some cases, based on small or unrepresentative samples. Nevertheless, the death of a child will inevitably take its toll on a marriage. "The difficulties associated with grief, fatigue, and other emotions that marital partners face following a child's death sometimes make it hard for them to understand one another, which tend to diminish communication and support," according to Brotherson. "Issues of concern in the marital relationship may include anger, irritability, need for privacy, and lack of understanding regarding one another's coping styles and expressions of grief."[3]

ADJUSTING EXPECTATIONS

No two parents will grieve the same. For some, grief is obvious and external. For others, it's obscure and internal. One spouse or partner may find relief in physical exercise, while the other may want to sit and read. One may want to be with friends, while the other craves solitude.

The timing of grief will differ also. One spouse or partner might be having a "good" day and doesn't feel overwhelmed with painful emotions. The other spouse may feel the opposite and want to talk about those feelings. One spouse may want to talk continually about the child who has died, which is hard for the other person who keeps memories unspoken because dialogue about the child causes pain. Differences like this can cause couples to feel out of sync with one another.

— ❧ —

"Give sorrow words; the grief that does not speak
knits up the o-er wrought heart and bids it break."[4]

William Shakespeare

— ❧ —

Alice: *I remember one day when Mark came home from work. It was about six weeks after Lora died. He had experienced a good day and felt productive at the office and with his patients. He was feeling positive. On the other hand, I'd had a depressing day with lots of "what if" feelings and wondering why this had to happen to our family. When I tried to share my feelings and find out how he was doing, he said, "I'm feeling OK, but this is bringing me down again." Other times, those roles were reversed. It was so hard to be on the same wavelength. You want to be understanding, but you also don't want to feel that same despair that your spouse or partner is experiencing. After a few months of this discord, we began to meet with a counselor. Having a mediator helped us work through these differences.*

Dr. Brotherson believes the demands of a marriage can add to the burden of pain following a child's death, and spouses may need to adjust their expectations of one another because everyone grieves differently. "Each spouse struggles with emotional and physical fatigue while trying to meet the continuing demands of life," he explains. Although relational difficulties may be magnified immediately following the death of a child, with time and adjustments the patterns of marriage resume. "Many couples report feeling better about their marriage than ever before because they have passed through the ultimate trial together and drawn closer."[5]

Three words that seem to stand out in Dr. Brotherson's comments are *demands*, *expectations*, and *adjustments*. Bills still need to be paid, dishes cleaned, meals prepared, pets fed, clothes washed, and other needs met. The simple and mundane acts of living continue whether you want them to or not. When couples feel numb and disconnected, one possible remedy is to simply make a list of what needs to be addressed that particular day. If you are both overwhelmed, which is likely, don't plan further than just that day. Decide who takes the garbage out or the kids to school or pays a bill. Adjusting can begin with small increments and result in finding your new normal as you figure out how to meet these demands. By having realistic expectations of the various demands that will be facing any couple following a loss, the adjustments may be smoother.

INTIMACY

Intimacy can be taking a walk together or sharing a deep conversation. It can be sharing dreams and fears and hopes or simply holding hands. There are many ways for a couple to be intimate. The apex of intimacy may occur during the act of sexual intercourse when needs are met and expressed by both involved in a satisfying way.

Sexual intimacy between couples may become difficult after the death of a child. The act that brought the child into the world may now seem threatening. The miraculous process of creating a human being has created the greatest pain imaginable. Why go through that again?

Fatigue, depression, low energy, numbness, and lack of confidence are more prevalent during grieving and do not often contribute to a successful intimate relationship. "Usually sexual intimacy deceases for some time following a child's death, and individuals vary widely in their readiness to resume this aspect of marital life,"[6] says Brotherson.

For others, sexual intimacy may be the very act that brings comfort and unity to a couple. The key ingredient for an intimate relationship is communication. Both partners need to express their needs and desires. In return, both partners need to be willing to listen to the other. Perhaps one partner expresses that he or she is not ready for sexual intimacy. After the death of a child, a person's emotions may feel totally out of control. By refusing to be sexually intimate, this individual may feel in control of at least one aspect of his or her life.

In this case, it's vital for the other partner to respect this situation. Force, manipulation, and disregard for an individual's feelings will only erode any chance of genuine intimacy. As trust develops between two people, both will feel a sense of safety and comfort that enhances the desire for intimacy. Time can once again play an important role in this development. Intimacy cannot be rushed, but it can be encouraged through kindness, loving gestures and words, open dialogue, feelings of calm, patience, a sense of trust, and time together.

— ⅔ —

"The goal is to have a conversation in a way
so that you can have another conversation tomorrow."

Unknown

— ⅔ —

HOW TO GRIEVE TOGETHER

As you journey through grief together with differing feelings and desires, here are a few action steps and things to remember that will help both of you:

1. Accept that your spouse or partner's method of grieving will be different from yours.
2. Accept that your spouse or partner may need his or her own space at times.
3. Make time to be together.
4. Listen when the other needs to share frustrations, anger, and heartbreak.
5. Apologize if you cause the other pain with your comments or actions.
6. Believe that a stronger and healthier relationship is possible.
7. Understand that blaming can be harmful.
8. Turn off phones, tablets, and computers and talk to one another.
9. Reflect on what brought you together in the first place.
10. Seek professional help if you are having difficulty with intimacy and communication.

TRY THIS
Try getting away as a couple from phones, computers, and other people. Go to a quiet restaurant or park. Or just sit in your car or on a blanket outside. Give each other five-minute increments to share feelings, using the words, "I feel. . . ." Let the other spouse or partner simply listen carefully. After one of you shares your thoughts in these five-minute increments, the other need only say, "Thank you for sharing." When you both have shared, discuss how this method of communication made you each feel.

Nikki: *Eric is a fixer, so it was difficult for him to just watch me suffer. Following Taylor's death, I wanted to talk and he didn't. His way of dealing was so different from mine that it was frustrating. Making him deal with it in my way was not helpful. Seeing a family counselor was not right for him. It works for many, but not for him. In retrospect, I realize that I shouldn't have pushed him into something he didn't want to do. Although counseling was and is important to my mental health, it was not his method of working through issues.*

We were able to communicate better when we asked each other, "How do you grieve?" My advice would be to explain to each other how you grieve so there is understanding. Support and respect the way each other grieves. Just because two people grieve differently doesn't make one spouse wrong and the other right. It just means you are different. You should talk about your fears and concerns with each other. It also helped us to initiate conversations about Taylor so we both knew the subject was not off-limits. Communication and respect are key. We came to respect the other's desire to not talk about the death if it was not the right time.

Blaming can be detrimental and harm a relationship. Be careful to not lash out in anger, because you can never rewind the clock and take back that outburst. We are all imperfect. Mistakes are made. Neither member of a relationship wanted the child to die. We decided early on that we would not blame one another. Do everything you can to keep your family together through this time. I want my family to be together forever. I want to see and be with Taylor again. Blaming will not get me there.

In summary, relationships under stress are not easy. They will need closer attention and more fortification. Madeleine L'Engle expressed this,

> No long-term marriage is made easily, and there have been times when I've been so angry or so hurt that I thought my love would never recover. And then, in the midst of near despair, something has happened beneath the surface. A bright little flashing fish of hope has flicked silver fins and the water is bright and suddenly I am returned to a state of love again—till next time. I've learned that there will always be a next time, and that I will submerge in darkness and misery, but that I won't stay submerged. And each time something has been learned under the waters; something has been gained; and a new kind of love has grown. The best I can ask for is that this love, which has been built on countless failures, will continue to grow. I can say no more than that this is mystery, and gift, and that somehow or other, through grace, our failures can be redeemed and blessed.[7]

THOUGHTS FROM OTHERS WHO HAVE LOST A CHILD

"I felt as though my husband and I were in sync at the hospital when our son was dying from cancer. We agreed on which treatments were right for him and what to do and say to the other children we were raising. Once our son passed away, we were no longer unified. We couldn't seem to agree on anything. We are still trying to figure this out. I was strong at the hospital but weak afterward. He had a hard time at the hospital but would be strong afterward. We just grieve drastically differently."

—Shelley Merrill, mother of Cameron Merrill (2010–2013)

"My spouse and I have had completely different ways of dealing with this. He turned to anger, heartache, and depression. He didn't want to face it head-on and go through the emotional roller coaster. I knew that way would not work for me. I definitely allowed myself to feel every emotion, but I knew that I couldn't let it tear me down or else I would be throwing my life away with the disease. I took a year to figure it all out and slowly come back to the light. I allow myself to have a bad day, to just cry, to fully feel it, and then I move on."

—Crystal McNutt, mother of Jackson McNutt
(2008–still living with a fatal disease)

"The death brought us closer at the time. We initially shared many tears together. But we grieved differently. I wanted to talk things out, and Daren was more closed. That was difficult."

—Elaine Forrest, mother of Megan Forrest (1985–2005)

"A very close friend sent us to a grief counselor for several visits in the first few weeks after our daughter's death. It made a huge difference to have someone with experience and practice in aiding people during the emotional issues that followed the death of our baby. Just being told right at the start that my husband and I would experience our grief differently and that how we expressed it could even change daily was helpful. The counselor also explained to us that how deeply we grieve is often related to how well we knew the deceased. My husband was a busy graduate student for Elena's brief five months of life. He had very little contact with her. I spent nearly every waking (and many sleeping) moments with her held tight to my body. It prepared him for the concept that I would have a harder time letting go and that I would feel her absence so much more profoundly."

—*Candida Marie Knight, mother of Elena Marie Knight (2009–2010)*

"When my younger sister died in 1987, my husband and I grieved very differently. Greg didn't need to talk about my sister's death, and I did. He would tell me that her pain was over, she was happier now, and that I didn't need to worry about her. Because he didn't need to talk, I turned to food. Some six months later, I was caught up in what I had done to myself and called a counselor friend who came immediately to the house. He suggested that I write letters to my sister who had died. I could leave them out on my desk and think about her stopping by to read them. This was wonderfully helpful to me. When Scott died three years later, we were aware that our grieving would be unique to each one of us. We grieved differently, but we tried to make sure that if one of us needed to talk, the other would listen."

—*Diane Merten, mother of Scott Merten (1973–1990)*

"My husband never questions what I need to do. He doesn't understand all my ways, and I don't understand all of his, but we try to give space and understanding. We agree that it is OK. We also try to lift each other up and over hurdles as they come. It's difficult when you are both down at the same time. It's been a strange road for us. When he couldn't do things, I could. When I couldn't, he could."

—*Gina Newcomb, mother of Jason Alan Newcomb (1980–2005)*

"I had no idea of my husband's limitless patience until our son Alex died. He said, 'This is your journey. You're doing it the way you need to do this.' My reaction was to try and honor his journey in the same manner."

—*Pat Newport, mother of Alex Newport-Berra (1981–2014)*

"Men and women grieve differently. I did find some books that talked about this and how an individual needs freedom to grieve in his or her own way. Hopefully, this works both ways. Also, if you have a child who is very ill, he or she will probably cling to the caregiving parent and seem to reject the other parent. And that is very hard on a grieving parent."

—*Susan Fisher, mother of Dallan Fisher (1988–1992)*

"My husband and I didn't understand one another's different ways of grieving. My divorce from Lane's father was inevitable and possibly was hastened but was not a direct result of Lane's death. For me, I learned that the loss of a husband to infidelity can't compare to the loss of a child."

—Karen Martin, mother of Lane Anthony Martin (1971–1982)

"I maintain that women grieve differently than men. The counselor we saw disagreed and wouldn't be gender specific, but since that's my experience, that's my reality. I think my husband internalized his grief more initially. We found it was helpful to give each other space. Regarding Lindsay's death, the experience seemed to bring us closer together. With Lynette's death, he knew that I was probably going to do the same things that helped me with Lindsay. We both realized that we wouldn't be ourselves for a while. We didn't determine how long that period of time was going to be."

—Shannna Miller, mother of Lindsay Miller (1978–1978)
and Lynette Miller (1981–2011)

"My husband and I take care to let the other do what is needed to survive. We talk about Sam and the entire situation and have the overall feeling that we understand each other. I think the hardest thing is working on the parts of grieving that we do not have in common. In the parts we don't share, I feel pretty isolated."

—Ann Lahr, mother of Sam Lahr (1989–2009)

NOTES

1. Mitch Albom, *Tuesdays With Morrie* (New York: Doubleday, 1997), 174.
2. Khalil Gibran, *The Prophet* (New York: Alfred A. Knopf, 1968), 15–16.
3. Sean E. Brotherson, *Parental Accounts of a Child's Death: Influences on Parental Identity and Behavior* (Corvallis: Oregon State University, 2000).
4. William Shakespeare, *MacBeth*, act IV, scene iii.
5. Sean E. Brotherson, *Parental Accounts of a Child's Death: Influences on Parental Identity and Behavior* (Corvallis: Oregon State University, 2000).
6. Ibid.
7. Madeleine L'Engle, *The Irrational Season* (San Francisco: Harper Publishers, 1983), 88.

10

SUPPORT FOR SURVIVING CHILDREN

*"Children sense and experience loss and grief from a
very young age. Even infants can sense when something is
amiss, someone is missing, or something has changed."*[1]

—Kirsti A. Dyer, MD, MS

THEIR GRIEF—AS REAL AS YOURS

This is our longest chapter. That's probably because we both felt compelled to try and understand what our children were going through when our daughters died. Lora had five siblings when she died, and Taylor had two sisters and one brother at the time of her death. These surviving children played a key role in helping us understand the grieving process.

If the child you lost had siblings, then your responsibilities as a parent are compounded in dealing with grief. Not only are you dealing with your personal grief, but also that of your surviving children. Their grief is just as real as yours, and their lives will be just as deeply impacted by the loss as yours.

As passengers on an airplane, we are told to put the oxygen mask first on our own face and then to focus on getting the oxygen mask on our child's face. This principle can apply to the survival tactics associated with grief. It's difficult to find strength to support anyone, even our own children, if we have no strength to support ourselves. So first, we need to suck in as much oxygen as we can and then go to our children and provide them with oxygen as well. This doesn't mean that we should expect our hearts and minds to be healed before we reach out to surviving children. In fact, when a death occurs in a family, the entire family needs oxygen as soon as possible.

GRIEF INDICATORS

Like adults, children will have unique, individual reactions to the death of a sibling. Studies have been done that help provide a general overview of how a child will think, feel, and act at a specific age in regards to their understanding of death. It also helps to know that following a death, children may experience temper tantrums, become aggressive, struggle with school assignments and learning, make demands, or regress to thumb-sucking and bed-wetting. By understanding that these reactions are normal, you'll be better equipped to exercise more patience and reassurance.

The following is a list of common ways that children might respond to a death:

- sadness
- denial, shock, and confusion
- anger and irritability
- inability to sleep
- nightmares
- loss of appetite
- fear of being alone
- frequent physical complaints such as stomachaches and headaches
- loss of concentration
- guilt over failure to prevent the loss
- depression or a loss of interest in daily activities and events
- acting much younger for an extended period or reverting to earlier behaviors (bed-wetting, baby talk, or thumb-sucking)
- boisterous play
- withdrawal from friends
- sharp drop in school performance or refusal to attend school
- excessively imitating or asking questions about the deceased or making repeated statements of wanting to join the deceased
- inventing games about dying
- humiliation or guilt over personal failure to prevent loss of life

There are ways to tell how a young child is dealing with the loss of their sibling. Play is an important indicator—it's a universal language among children. Playing demonstrates a great deal about children because they project their inner selves through their actions. Drawing is also a valuable form of communication for young children. Their drawings tell a great deal about them because they often project feelings and emotions.

Nikki: *About five months after Taylor's death, Natalie was drawing pictures of Taylor. They were disturbing to me because Taylor was only a large head with a sad face and tears running down her cheeks. I asked Natalie to explain her drawing, and she said that Taylor doesn't have a body because she is in heaven, and she is sad because she is hurt and misses us. This was concerning to me. So we sat and talked about all the things that this picture depicted. I could tell that Natalie believed that Taylor was still in pain from the car accident. We talked about how she is no longer in pain. We talked about all the things that were troubling her, none of which I would have figured out right away if she hadn't drawn this picture. Soon after our talk, Natalie would draw Taylor with a body and a more proportionate head. The pictures were happy and had color. I could tell healing had begun.*

My three children all expressed their grief differently over Taylor's death. Natalie's grief was evident at night. She would start to panic and miss her sister so much. She suffered from extreme nightmares. During the first ten months, she would wake up about an hour after she fell asleep and start screaming. While still asleep, she would actually reenact the experience of seeing her little sister hit by a car. She would say nonsense words or shout out phrases like "Mommy's crying, police, blood!" She would even reach out and try to grab her sister and pull her out of the way of the car. Upon awaking in the morning, she had no memory of the nightmare.

As parents, it was traumatic and exhausting for us to see our daughter going through this experience over and over. It was disturbing. I actually got to the point where I told my husband that I couldn't do another night of this torture. I just felt like giving up. Initially, I kept waking her up during her nightmare to stop the trauma. I later learned from a professional that Natalie's young mind needed to go through the motions to process the terror associated with the event. We took this advice, and the nightmares ended about ten months after Taylor's death.

Regression is normal for children. Before the death of Taylor, Alivia was fully potty trained. After Taylor's death, Alivia started wetting the bed every night for the next year. She even went back to crawling on the ground, sucking on her little sister's pacifiers, and saying that she would be Taylor so I won't be sad.

Tyson's reaction was more quiet and reserved. He came to my husband and me a couple of weeks after the funeral and told us, "Mom and Dad, you need to keep it together. I'll be just fine as long as you keep it together." Not what I expected to hear from a seven-year-old. He was right though. He handled everything really well until one of us got weepy, and then Tyson would burst into tears and go lay in bed.

HELPING CHILDREN GRIEVE

Children need to be allowed to talk about the deceased. There may be times when you wish they would not speak about their sibling, but try hard not to squelch their need to talk. Encourage the conversation. Listen without judgment. At the same time, give them space and time if they do not want to talk. Different children will have different ways of expressing their grief. Even within the same family, one sibling may need to draw pictures to work through their grief, while another brother or sister will find relief in solitude. Another will want to be surrounded by family members and involved in dialogue. There is no wrong or right way to grieve, no matter what the age. Let them ask questions.

Alice: *If you have younger children, you may be blown away by the questions they will ask about death. Treat each question with dignity. If you laugh or scoff or minimize their question, they will stop asking, and that can hinder their grieving process. Some of the comments and questions from our children after Lora died of cancer included the following:*

- *Sara, at age 5: "My tennis shoes might drown if I wash them too much. Tennis shoes are alive too."*
- *Sara, at age 5: "If Lora is a little girl in heaven, how will I get to play with her when I die, because I'll be grown up?"*
- *Anna, at age 8: "Everyone has cancer in them a little, and Lora's just grew. We have to figure out how to stop it growing."*
- *Anna, at age 8: "My face feels fat today. Do I have cancer too?"*
- *Marcus, at age 10: "Do you think something went wrong when your egg and Dad's sperm came together?"*
- *Meta, at age 11: "Why did God make Lora die?"*

And there's the classic comment by Sara, as written in my journal:

> *One morning when I was sad and feeling no energy, five-year-old Sara crawled in bed with me and asked me why I was sad. I told her that I missed Lora. She looked me straight in the eye and said, "I will be Lora." It hit me how this beautiful little Sara Jean was at risk for losing her own identity, so I told her that I already had a Lora and she had died. I only wanted her to be Sara and that I loved her just as she was. It's so important to make sure that our children don't try to "become" the deceased sibling. They need to be who they are and meet their own individual potential, no matter how much we miss the child who has died.*

Individual and family counseling is always an option to help children through the grieving process. Sometimes a child will find it more comfortable to express their thoughts to a person who is not related to the family. Seek out a good grief counselor by asking for recommendations from your family physician or health care provider; other parents who have gone through a loss; a school counselor; the religious leader of your church, mosque, or synagogue; or an organization that deals with grief, such as hospice.

Another thing to consider is the gender of the counselor. This may or may not be a factor. Your son may not talk to a female counselor, but if given the opportunity, he may open up to a male counselor. Similarly, your daughter may only want to talk with a female counselor.

Kristi A. Dyer, MD, MS, is a physician and facilitator on death, dying, and bereavement. Her website, JourneyofHearts.org, addresses loss and significant life changes, helping those who are grieving. When communicating with children about death, she recommends the following points:

- Use concrete terms when explaining death. Avoid terms such as *passed on* or *went to sleep*. Children may not understand that these terms mean the person has died.
- Answer their questions about death simply and honestly. Only offer details that they can absorb. Try not to overload them with information.
- Allow children to attend the funeral if they want to, but do not force it. Let them know what to expect at the funeral.
- Give children alternatives for using their grief positively—drawing, other creative means of expression, writing letters, reading, or writing poetry and stories.
- Make sure your child doesn't feel at fault.

- Give children choices in what they do or don't do to remember the deceased. Allow children to participate in the family rituals if they want to—going to the funeral or cemetery, helping plan the ceremony, picking flowers, and so on.
- Allow children to talk about the deceased, but don't push them to talk about their feelings.
- Be aware that children need time to grieve and be upset. Let them know you are available to listen when they are ready to talk. Provide reassurance and validate their feelings when they express them.
- The family's spiritual beliefs about death should be explained in simple terms. However, children may not understand the meaning, and although they can repeat what was said, they may still not comprehend what death means.
- Children can be fearful about death. Give them a chance to talk about their fears and listen when they express their fears.
- Be patient. It may take them a long time to recover from their loss.
- Expect that their grief may recur throughout their childhood or adolescence. Strong reminders, such as the anniversary of a death, a birthday, or a celebration without the loved one may reawaken grief. Be available to talk.
- Children may even mourn the loss of environment that existed before the death; they grieve the "changed" behavior. It can be helpful to keep to regular routines.

TRY THIS
Ask your child(ren) to write down or to draw their memories of their brother or sister who has died. Keep these in a notebook and refer to them as a family once a year.

Nikki: *Your child may have a difficult time determining reality versus imagination. Eric and I took our children to Disneyland seven months after the death of Taylor so we could spend some quality time together. Now, just imagine a six- and a four-year-old meeting Cinderella for the first time, and she tells them that if you wish upon a star, all of your dreams come true. It was heartbreaking to go back to the hotel that night with the girls believing that their dreams of Taylor coming alive could come*

*true. I felt like going up to Cinderella and slapping the pretty little smile off
her face. I ached having to explain reality to these little girls. I was not happy
to burst that bubble, but I didn't want them to have an expectation that
would never be met.*

Many families find that talking about heaven can be a great way to
help children deal with the loss. It's helpful for children to envision a
place of peace. Heaven can have many definitions, but one that resonates
with children is a place where their loved one is not in pain, disabled, or
suffering the trials of mortality.

Nikki: *My children's definitions of heaven were all different. Tyson (seven)
believes that in heaven, Taylor can run all day and all night and not get tired.
It helps children to imagine the best possible scenario and put their sibling
there. For a seven-year-old boy, never getting tired would be the best place
ever. Natalie (five) imagines Taylor in a place that has cotton candy clouds
and video games that you can play without asking permission. Alivia (three)
thinks of heaven as an all-you-can-eat ice cream bar, where the counters are
only two feet tall so you can get to the ice cream anytime you want, without
help. She envisions reaching up and grabbing the stars and putting them in
her hair as hair clips. What a beautiful thought! By expounding and validat-
ing their ideas, you can help your child deal with the loss as their imagination
can stretch to the ends of the world. Go ahead and ask your children, "What
is your ideal place? What would you be able to do there? What do you eat?
What toys do you play with?" Try to keep answers positive and specific to that
child's interests.*

As parents who have lost a child, we can share with each other ways to
support our surviving children. We can also tap into research throughout
the world dealing with children and grief. What we think is abnormal
may be a very common occurrence with children who have lost a sibling.
By becoming familiar with how a child understands death, we can better
understand how to help our surviving children cope with the death of
their sibling.

This table was adapted from a nursing school curriculum using information from Louise M. Aldrich's highly regarded work *Sudden Death:
Crisis in the School.*[2] This table discusses children (ages three through
twelve) and their thoughts, emotions, and resulting actions when faced
with a death.

PROCESSES ASSOCIATED WITH DEATH IN CHILDREN, AGES THREE THROUGH TWELVE

AGE	THOUGHTS	EMOTIONS	ACTIONS
3–5	Death can be reversed and is not permanent. Death might be confused with trips or time asleep. Some curiosity about the deceased's whereabouts and activities.	Anger Sadness Anxiety Withdrawal Fear Crankiness	Bed-wetting Crying Fighting Preoccupation with things relating to death Acting as though the death never happened
6–9	Death is final. There are biologic processes associated with death. There is an association of death with mutilation. Ghosts or spirits took the deceased. What will happen if their parent(s) dies and who will take care of them? Some concern that the death is a result of their actions or words.	Anger Sadness Anxiety Withdrawal Fear Crankiness Confusion about changes (Emotions may be demonstrated during play.)	Aggressive behavior Withdrawal from others Nightmares Night terrors Pretend that death did not happen Lack of concentration Decline in school performance

continued on next page

continued from previous page

9–12	Death is final. Death is hard to talk about. There is anxiousness that death will reoccur. Facetiousness or joking about death helps make it easier. What will happen if their parent(s) dies, and who will take care of them? There is concern that the death is a result of their actions or words.	Anger Sadness Anxiety Vulnerability Fear Confusion about changes Loneliness Abandonment Guilt Worry Isolation	Aggressive behavior Withdrawal from others Nightmares Night terrors Talk about physical aspects of death Pretend that death did not happen Refrain from showing emotions Lack of concentration Decline in school performance
12 and older (teen-agers)	Death is final. Showing emotions is weakness. There is a need to be in control of feelings. Facetiousness or joking about death helps make it easier. There is concern about life before and after death. There is concern that the death is a result of their actions or words.	Same as 9–12-year-olds Anger Sadness Anxiety Vulnerability Fear Confusion about changes Loneliness Abandonment Guilt Worry Isolation	Aggressive behavior Nightmares Argumentative outbursts Screaming Fighting Placing themselves in precarious situations Grief over what might have been Pretense that it never happened Lack of concentration Decline in school performance

Dr. Suresh K. Joishy, a hematologist in Fresno, California, is the author of the medical textbook *Palliative Medicine Secrets*.[3] The book prepares physicians for treating dying children and the questions they will ask. Palliative care includes the psychological, emotional, social, and spiritual well-being of a patient.

Joishy has studied end-of-life care in patients around the world. He has found that up to age two, a child's world is formed by sensory information. Children will be aware of tension and impending separation. They are comforted by the presence of loved ones and by touching, rocking, and their favorite toys.

From age two to six, children have a concept that is close to "magical thinking"—death is not permanent, and they don't believe it could happen to them. It may help them to learn more concrete information and that death is not sleep.

Children age seven to twelve are aware that death is final and that it *can* happen to them. They may ask specifics, including about burial. Many are able to hear and cope with details of their illness.

Adolescents older than twelve may act out and rebel, yet at the same time feel distanced from the death process. They may want to speak about the future they'll never see and experiences they will miss, including college, career, marriage, and having children.

Alice: *It can be difficult when you have a child with serious injuries or a disease or cancer and you ask their siblings to think good thoughts and pray for the ailing brother or sister. Our children prayed nightly for six months that Lora would be cured of cancer. They exercised hope and faith in their own individual ways. When she died, it was as though their prayers hadn't been answered. That necessitated many conversations on what faith is and how we can hope for something, but it doesn't always go the way we wish. Life, with all of its twists and turns, still happens. The positive that comes out of this is that children who have undergone a major loss, while young, have a resilience that will sustain them at other times in their lives.*

Above all, recognize that your children will grieve. Ignoring their personal grief may result in problems later. Become aware of what you can do to understand their grief and to offer them comfort, nurturing, unconditional love, and support.

— ⁊ —

"Weeping is perhaps the most human and
universal of all relief measures."

Dr. Karl Menninger

— ⁊ —

THOUGHTS FROM OTHERS WHO HAVE LOST A CHILD

"Siblings can be asked to help in significant ways, especially if they are older. Our two children, McHale and Adam, wrote the piece for the newspaper about their brother's life. They both spoke at our 'Gatherings to Honor Alex' and the entire family was involved in how to honor Alex with the funds from the Alex Newport-Berra FUNdation. Adam published a book of Alex's poems and also set up a website (AlexNewportBerra.com) to honor his brother where friends could add their messages and photos. McHale ran her first 5K as Alex had once encouraged her. She is now training for her third and feels that this is her time with Alex. It's important to honor and respect the way our children choose to grieve and not suggest they do their journey in a specific way."

—*Pat Newport, mother of Alex Newport-Berra (1981–2014)*

"Our children never knew their older sister, Lindsay, who died before they were born. I have a little trunk with some of Lindsay's things, and on her birthday I would take those out and also show them her special photo album. It was healing to talk about her during these times. We would also visit the cemetery and leave flowers for her. . . .

"When Lynette died, my husband and I endeavored to be a sounding board for our surviving children. They shared their anger that Lynette died from something that was preventable. In July 2012, we rented a house for a week at our favorite beach on the Oregon coast. We called it Christmas in July. Carynn, Bret, Melinda, their spouses, and two grandsons joined us for a week of healing, playing, crying, and family time. It was one of the best things we could have done for all of us."

—*Shanna Miller, mother of Lindsay Miller (1978–1978) and Lynette*
Miller (1981–2011)

"After our son's funeral, my husband and I shared with our daughter how much we admired and appreciated her support during Jas's illness. She had put herself last in order for Jas to be first so much of her life. She was able to talk about growing up with a brother who had a terminal illness and what it meant in her life. We explained that she would find it difficult to find a new place to exist. She would miss her brother and at the same time, she would now be an only child. It would be new, it would be great, and it was going to hurt like heck—the missing and the guilt both. I let her know that if she needed to talk to someone to help figure things out, I was right there for her. Nothing was taboo. If she needed someone professional, I would help her find that too."

—*Gina Newcomb, mother of Jas Newcomb (1980–2005)*

"Tell them to let the tear out. Hold them when they cry. Make sure they realize their sibling is not in pain and that we will all live together someday when our missions on earth are accomplished."

—*Shelley Merrill, mother of Cameron Merrill (2010–2013)*

"It's really still a blur as to what we did or didn't do for our children. To this day, I do not know how Cindy and Nicole (two older sisters) dealt with the loss of their brother. That breaks my heart. This is my biggest regret. I found out years later that Jennifer (younger sister) was silent about her grief for a whole year until one day when I sat down beside her and asked how she was doing. She was able to open up and start to heal. I let her suffer in silence for a whole year? I regret sending Cory (older brother) back to college the day of the funeral. I felt it was important for him to get right back to his regular schedule. Maybe that is not what he needed. Maybe he needed to drop out of that semester and be home and cared for. Our eldest son was serving a mission for The Church of Jesus Christ of Latter-day Saints. We were able to talk to him by telephone. We knew he was going to be OK because we were able to have that conversation. The only advice I can give is to make sure each child knows that you know that they exist and that they are loved just as much as the child who has passed away. Help them realize that it's OK to be happy and have wonderful daily experiences."

—*Debora Eichelberger, mother of Dustin Guy Eichelberger (1985–2000)*

"When Hannah passed away, our other children were Meagan (eighteen), Ryan (thirteen), Katie (eleven), and Zachary (two and a half). They each had their own special relationship with their sister. We took them to counseling for a short time because of the circumstances of Hannah's death and the fact that we didn't know what to do. Gary and I had never done this before; we were at a loss. We found that the older kids didn't want to talk much about how they were feeling. They did, however, express some of their feelings through writing poems and drawing pictures. Zachary spent all his time with Hannah; his little brain just couldn't understand what was going on and why she didn't come home from the hospital. He would ask me why I left her there. Gary and I eventually had to take him to the hospital to show him that Hannah wasn't there. Zachary talked about Hannah all the time and still does. For the first two years, Zachary would ask me several times a day where Hannah was. I would have to explain to him over and over again in different ways where she was. As he's gotten older he understands better, and his questions are different. The biggest thing was to make sure all the kids knew that I was always there, and they could—day or night—come and talk, cry, or whatever they needed to do. They are all still working through their grief in their own ways. I put framed pictures of Hannah in each of their rooms. They have something that reminds them of special times with their sister."

—*Brenda Kingsley, mother of Hannah Marie Kingsley (2004–2009)*

"We had four surviving sons, ages five, four, three, and a newborn. We told our children that Wendy was with Heavenly Father now, and we would see her again. Initially, that seemed to satisfy them. However, Greg, the three-year-old, seemed to be restless and unable to focus the morning of the third day. He came to me and said, 'Can I go to Heavenly Father's house?' It broke my heart. I knew he was missing his little sister with whom he loved to play. He quit eating for a week, and he had nightmares for several months. I felt like I didn't do anything special, but I made sure they knew they were loved."

—*Nadine Nielsen King, mother of Wendy Lynne Nielsen (1960–1961)*

"We tried to make sure we included my older son's friends in vacations and activities, but I feel I didn't do so well with his loss. Bereavement is a selfish process because individuals are so focused on their own pain and trying to find a reason for a child's death. Guilt was a paramount, paralyzing condition for me."

—*Karen Martin, mother of Lane Anthony Martin (1971–1982)*

"At the time of Dallan's death, we had four other children who were nine, seven, five, and one-and-a-half years old. Scott and I felt that we should always be honest about Dallan's cancer. When we found out that he was not going to live, we told the other children. We used the example of a hand (the soul or spirit) and a glove (the body) to explain our concept of life and death. When the glove is on the hand, it has the ability to move and wiggle. When it is separated from the hand, it lies lifeless, but the hand still continues to move and returns to heaven. I wasn't sure our five-year-old daughter understood this concept. I asked her the next day if she had understood, and she replied, 'Yes, you said that Dallan is going to live back with Heavenly Father. Isn't that what we all want to do?' That was a lesson to me! Children do grieve differently both from each other and from adults. You have to give them their space to do so. I think we should have had more counseling for our older children. The school did some, but you can't assume that because they are not vocal they are not still suffering from the loss. It can be the cause of other negative behaviors."

—Susan Fisher, mother of Dallan Fisher (1988–1992)

"I let them bring up his death, address the question, and then redirect the topic to something about them that they are good at or enjoy. I always tell them to let the tears out, and I ask, 'Can I hug you while you let the tears out?' There's a difference between asking 'What can I do to help you feel better?' and 'Can I hug you while you let the tears out?' I try to picture that Cameron has a new, perfect body in heaven now. He doesn't have any more 'owies' or 'tubies.' Our work is to love God and help people and learn. When we finish our work here on earth, we will be able to join Cameron. He just finished his work early. I give the children lots of cuddles. I allow myself to cry in front of them, and I simply say, 'Mommy will cry for a little while, but then I will stop and it's OK.'"

—Shelley Merrill, mother of Cameron Merrill (2010–2013)

"I was very open with our twenty-seven-month-old daughter, Elena's big sister, as to how I was grieving. I never tried to hide my tears from her. When I would cry, I would offer her my arms and as I held her, I would tell her that I missed baby Elena. That I missed having her in our house. I didn't want her to think that these sad feelings were something that we need to hide from others."

—Candida Marie Knight, mother of Elena Marie Knight (2009–2010)

"Scott and his younger brother, Paul, were really great friends. They created games and played them; they made plans reading *Architectural Digest* magazine about what their apartment together would look like. When Scott died, I did not have the emotional stamina to give to my children as I had before his death. I was able to prepare meals, help with laundry, and drive them to their athletic practices and games, but not much more. Paul started sixth grade, and my neglect of his needs became very apparent when he brought home a report card with an F in his science class. I had not even known that he was failing the class. I realized the need to rise again and strive to be a dedicated and helpful mother. My children needed this, and so did I."

—Diane Merten, mother of Scott Merten (1973–1990)

"When Lora died, we wondered if the timing was right to have another child. No additional child could ever replace Lora, but we still felt a nagging that our family was not complete and we did not want a huge gap between our living children and a new baby. We also recognized that our children's lives had been emotionally impacted with the death of their little sister. Like us, they felt a lack of control in their lives. So we chose to have this be a family decision. We went to the children and explained that we were considering having another child. Four of the five children were ecstatic, but eight-year-old Anna had reservations. She was not ready. So we told her to tell us when she was ready. A few weeks later, she came to us and said that she was ready for another baby in the family now. Making this a family decision was the right thing to do."

—Mark Rampton, father of Lora Rampton (1984–1986)

NOTES

1. Kirsti A. Dyer. Quoted in "Helping Children Cope with Death." Journey Of Hearts. Accessed May 22, 2015. http://www.journeyofhearts.org/grief/kids_death.html
2. Louise M. Aldrich, *Sudden Death: Crisis in the School* (Ramona, CA: Cherry Hill, 1996)
3. Suresh K. Joishy, *Palliative Medicine Secrets* (Hanley and Belfus, 1999).
4. Karl Menninger, quoted in Bernard Nisenholz *Sigmund Says: And Other Psychotherapists' Quotes* (Lincoln: iUniverse, 2006), 154.

11

FAITH AND HOPE

"Hope is like light. . . . even the tiniest bit guides us through the darkness."

—Unknown

A TIME FOR DIFFICULT QUESTIONS

A child who loses his or her parents is called an orphan. A woman who loses her husband is called a widow. A man who loses his wife is called a widower. There is no word in the English language for a parent who loses a child—it's just unnatural. This can lead to questions.

Many individuals ask, "Why did God let this happen?" Some questions may never have an answer that brings comfort and closure. Realizing that there might not be a satisfactory answer to your question at this time may be helpful.

One woman's son died in an accident when he was walking along a dark road and was hit by a car. The mother went repeatedly to her religious leaders, asking "Why did this happen?" After months of trying to get the answer to this question, she was simply told, "God did not make this happen. Your son was walking on a dark road and was hit by a car, and he died." It's harsh, but it's reality. Accepting reality is part of healing.

Deep reflections on life, afterlife, and God are common when someone dies. The role of spirituality or religion in a time of loss is universal. It's common to search religious beliefs for answers to the questions, "What happens to our loved ones when they die?" or "Will I ever see them again?"

Alice's journal entry April 24, 1986 (three months after Lora's death):
All deaths are difficult, but I agree with the experts now that the death of a person's child is especially hard. When you bury an old person, you bury

85

achievements, learning, experiences, a long life, and so on, but when you bury a child, you bury their dreams, future, potential. And with a baby, like Lora, you also bury someone you're not sure you really knew. Even a twelve-year-old would have had a more definite personality. I am frustrated because I'm not really certain who Lora was going to become. It's like an identity crisis relating to her now. Is her spirit grown? Is she a baby? Am I her mother? Am I her sister? Does she need me anymore? If I were to see her, who would I see? I've prayed for a sure knowledge that she is all right but have not received what I think I need. Will I ever? Do I have to be more patient or have more faith or not expect a miracle? Sometimes I feel anger at God. Why does it have to be a game of hide-and-seek with those who have died? Why can't I just see Lora again? Life is hard to figure out. Basically, I do OK each day. I keep busy, and I know that life must go on. But sometimes this life seems so void and purposeless. The other day I saw a man pruning his hedge, and he looked so ridiculous at the time. I wondered, "Why do people prune hedges?" "Why does so much of what we do seem unimportant?" I simply long for a more complete peace. I long for an assurance of Lora's spiritual existence.

Trials squeeze the artificial out of us, and raw emotions can leave us feeling vulnerable because our bare souls are there for all to see. We question what we believe and what our lives mean. But often, by working through adversity, we come to more clearly define life. Throughout history, people have tried to come to terms with the subject of death. You are experiencing feelings that have been felt by grieving parents since the beginning of time. In this chapter, we share some thoughts that have given us comfort. Borrow from us or seek to find your own source of strength.

FAITH IN SOMETHING MORE

People have their own ideas, beliefs, faith, religions, and ways of dealing with the unnatural. We are not here to say one is more right than another. If faith and hope can bring solace to your soul, then tap into that power.

— ❧ —

"I do not understand the mystery of grace—only that it meets us where we are and does not leave us where it found us."[1]

Anne Lamott

— ❧ —

For many, religious beliefs have softened the blow of death and provided an eternal perspective. Across cultures worldwide, people have found common beliefs in their understanding of death. Almost all of the various faiths believe that death is a transition to another state of being.

Faith can bring hope, but the opposite can happen as well. You may feel anger toward God or have feelings of being robbed of time and end up turning away from your religion or faith. The two extremes and everything in between can be found in grieving parents.

Broken hearts can heal. Faith can be the hope you need to help heal a broken heart in ways you might not be able to imagine. But before a wound can heal, the injured must recognize they are bleeding. Once that happens, the individual can move forward.

— ❧ —

"Someday it will all make sense . . . someday."

Unknown

— ❧ —

Nikki: *Move forward in faith. Cling to any faith you have so you can have hope again. Hope that you will see your child again. Hope that you will be happy again. Hope that your pain will ease. If you feel you have no faith, then "borrow" from someone else until you have the strength to hold on for yourself. Faith was a huge part of my grieving process. Having faith doesn't mean that if you live a good life you won't suffer. But it does mean that when life happens, you have a way to handle it. Often we do not know what we can handle until after the trial of our faith. Like our earthly parents, God doesn't always protect us from all aches and pain. Personally, I believe Jesus Christ is my Savior and that he is the Savior of all, including Taylor. He also went through pain beyond comparison and died for all. I believe that life is fair because Jesus Christ was willing to bear it too. If you have asked the question, Why me?, then I would ask you, Why not you? Through our trials we come to know and feel of God's love. Sometimes He lets it rain so we can appreciate the sun.*

There is no perfect answer or solution to dealing with grief. Faith may be one of the steps that can help in your healing process. Sometimes after a death we need to start at ground zero with our faith so we can eventually regain hope in our lives. We may need to rely on those with faith if ours is weak or diminished. Small steps to regain our faith may include prayer, meditation, patience, reading faith-based literature and scriptures, or talking to inspired leaders. Regaining faith can be an important tool in gaining a hope for a humane world again.

SCRIPTURES AND OTHER WORDS OF INSPIRATION

Studying the words of inspired individuals born twenty or two thousand years ago may be something to consider. Thoughts of inspiration can come to all of us, but fortunately, many wise individuals took time to put those feelings down on paper, thus lifting others for generations.

The Christian faith offers words of comfort in Christ's Sermon on the Mount, found in the New Testament: "Blessed are they that mourn: for they shall be comforted" (Matthew 5:4). Later, Christ says, "Come unto me, all ye that labour and are heavy laden, and I will give you rest. Take my yoke upon you, and learn of me; for I am meek and lowly in heart: and ye shall find rest unto your souls. For my yoke is easy, and my burden is light" (Matthew 11:28–30).

The Hindu *Bhagavad Gita* offers comfort in its description of the soul: "As a man casts off worn-out garments and puts on new ones, so the embodied soul casts off the worn-out body and enters other new ones. No weapon can cleave him; nor the fire burn him, no waters can make him wet, nor the wind dry him up. Uncleaveable is he; he is not burnt; nor be wetted and neither be dried; eternal, all-pervading, stable, and immovable is he from everlasting time."[2]

Throughout history, millions have turned to faith-based words for solace such as found in the twenty-third Psalm from the Hebrew Bible, or Old Testament: "The Lord is my shepherd; I shall not want. He maketh me to lie down in green pastures: he leadeth me beside the still waters. He restoreth my soul: he leadeth me in the paths of righteousness for his name's sake. Yea, though I walk through the valley of the shadow of death, I will fear no evil: for thou art with me; thy rod and thy staff they comfort me. Thou preparest a table before me in the presence of mine enemies: thou anointest my head with oil; my cup runneth over. Surely goodness and mercy shall follow me all the days of my life: and I will dwell in the house of the Lord forever."[3]

From the writings of Buddha, we learn, "A place to stay untouched by death does not exist. It does not exist in space, it does not exist in the ocean, nor if you stay in the middle of a mountain. If you accept that death is part of life, then when it actually does come, you may face it more easily."[4]

Lao-Tzu (Laozi) was a philosopher and poet of ancient China and thought to be the founder of philosophical Taoism. He lived at least four hundred to five hundred years BCE. One of his writings provokes an image that a shortened life can have as much light and influence as one that is long: "The flame that burns twice as bright burns half as long."[5]

Chapter seventy five, verses 36–40, of the Qur'an of Islam, addresses life after life: "Does man think that he is to be left purposeless? Was he not a drop of fluid emitted forth? Then he became a clot and then Allah shaped and proportioned him, and He made of him a pair, male and female. Has not such a One the power to bring the dead to life?"

Abdu'l-Baha, an early leader and scholar in the Baha'i faith, gave numerous talks and answered questions of visitors to Haifa, Israel, during the early 1900s. In describing the separation of the spirit from the body at the time of death, Abdu'l-Baha used this beautiful analogy: "To consider that after the death of the body the spirit perishes is like imagining that a bird in a cage will be destroyed if the cage is broken, though the bird has nothing to fear from the destruction of the cage. Our body is like the cage, and the spirit is like the bird. . . . If the cage becomes broken, the bird will continue to exist. Its feelings will be even more powerful, its perceptions greater, and its happiness increased."[6]

Others have found strength in words from modern-day religious leaders like the Dalai Lama who has written the following: "Analysis of death is not for the sake of becoming fearful but to appreciate this precious lifetime during which you can perform many important practices. Rather than being frightened, you need to reflect that when death comes, you will lose this good opportunity for practice. In this way contemplation of death will bring more energy to your practice."[7]

Grief is not new. We can read words dating over two thousand years regarding Adam and Eve grieving the death of their son Abel. The written word through the ages gives us examples of those who have lost loved ones and still found hope.

HOPE

Faith is a medium in which hope can take root and grow. Imagine a garden in which you have planted seed. You have no certainty that anything will grow, but faith is what gave you the impetus to plant the seed. Hope is the belief that if you wait long enough, your seeds will become plants. Faith and hope are synonymous with optimism, and if we hope for growing and healing, they are more likely to happen.

— ❧ —

"We must accept finite disappointment, but
we must never lose infinite hope."[8]

Martin Luther King

— ❧ —

Nikki: *I was lamenting one day that I didn't have much video footage of Taylor. I was flipping through my phone and I found two pretty lengthy videos that she had taken of herself. I had no idea they were there. She must have been playing with my phone one day and put it on video and captured almost every ounce of herself. It was sweet and precious to me. I felt I had been given a gift from God. He knew my needs.*

— ❧ —

"Where there is great love, there are always miracles."[9]

Willa Cather

— ❧ —

If we look, we may recognize divine intervention in our lives, which will help us on the path to faith and hope. We all have access to a personal "toolbox," which contains instruments to help us deal with grief. We go to our toolbox in time of need. Each tool represents something to give us strength and hope. They may include

- living for your remaining family members
- living your life in a way that would make your deceased child proud
- taking time to pray
- developing faith and hope
- finding enjoyment and success in the workplace
- helping others get through the stages of grief
- giving service
- finding fellowship by worshipping at a church, mosque, synagogue, or in a special place that is sacred to you
- relying on the strength of others
- remembering the art of gratitude

Nikki: *I'm convinced that the Lord may push us to the very brink of despair to test who our God really is. He tests us to see who we turn to in our hour of need. He blesses our lives, and then we can turn and express gratitude for those blessings. I don't think I've ever been grateful for my trials, but I'm grateful for what I learn from them. I'm grateful for the tender mercies that I see because of my trials.*

In the book entitled *Maximum Brain Power: Challenging the Brain for Health and Wisdom* by Shlomo Breznitz and Collins Hemingway, we discover, "The brain does not want the body to expend its resources unless we have a reasonable chance of success. Our physical strength is not accessible to us if the brain does not believe in the outcome, because the worst possible thing for humans to do is to expend all of our resources and fail. If we do not believe we can make it, we will not get the resources we need to make it. The moment we believe, the gates are opened, and a flood of energy is unleashed. Both hope and despair are self-fulfilling prophecies."

Feeling hopelessness after losing a child is normal. Your purpose for living is challenged. What you thought you knew about life, love, and your beliefs may be dashed to pieces; it takes time to put the pieces back together and feel whole. Faith and hope provide tools to help us look beyond the pain and ponder the possibility of life and living beyond death.

THOUGHTS FROM OTHERS WHO HAVE LOST A CHILD

"The scientific part of me says that if you want to find a pattern you will. If you want to see a pattern of anger, hurt, and pain in your life, you will. If you want to see a pattern of miracles, love, and spiritual help, you can find it. I wouldn't say I am religious, but I would say I'm spiritual. I try to look for the good. I acknowledge that if there is a God, He put people in my path to help me get through this tragedy in the smoothest way possible."

—*Cressey Merrill, father of Cameron Merrill (2010–2013)*

TRY THIS
Find a book that gives you hope for a brighter day. This could be the scriptures, inspirational poetry, or a book by an author who has experienced grief also. Strengthen yourself by learning of their experiences.

"Part of me died when Cameron died. I'm trying to fit that 'partial person' into this new life full of obstacles and painful moments to overcome. I just hang onto the time when I get to see God and see Cameron. I have no idea how God will unite our family in a way that it will all be healed and happy, but I have faith he can fill that tall order! That is what makes it better for me after a year of life without Cameron."

—*Shelley Merrill, mother of Cameron Merrill (2010–2013)*

"These are thoughts that have helped me over the years:

Peace does not mean to be in a place where there is no noise, trouble, or hard work. It means to be in the midst of those things and still be calm in your heart.

- Sometimes we need a 'rough patch' to help us prioritize.
- Most of us have had or will have trials.
- It's important to pray always.
- Recognize the power of the Holy Ghost and then trust that witness.
- Do we pay the price to get answers to our prayers?
- Prayer is a passport to spiritual strength.
- We can be more than the adversities we face."

—*Cammy Wilberger, mother of Brooke Wilberger (1985–2004)*

"I've learned that our capacity to endure the loss of a son is largely determined by two factors. One is our willingness to accept, i.e., have faith that there is a personal God who is involved in our lives and whose will or intention takes precedence over ours and we surrender to that will. The second is the assurance that death is but a temporary separation and the reunion will be a joyful one."

—*Greg Merten, father of Scott Frederick Merten (1973–1990)*

"I am thankful for a belief system in which I know I will be with Megan again and she will be free from her disabilities and frustrations with life. I'm grateful for people in my life who were able to lift me up. If you need help, find somebody to talk to. It might be a friend, family member, clergy, or professional. Just find someone. It's important."

—*Elaine Forrest, mother of Megan Forrest (1985–2005)*

"Immediately after World War II, I visited several families of my close friends who had been killed in action. Without exception, they reached out for anything I could tell them about the last days and manner of death of their beloved. Without question, religion helped some of them cope; to me, it seemed a godsend for them. For me, recalling our time together and Craig's brief life as an adult is solace. I enjoy reminiscing about him with family and friends."

—Craig Leman, father of Craig A. Leman (1956–1998)

"My daughter had a severe heart defect: actually, several. Her oxygen saturation was low. If she was out in the cold, she would start to turn blue. She had poor circulation. Her body was oxygen starved. I picture Hannah in heaven with a new heart and a new life. No pain. She is happy, healthy, and complete. I miss her terribly, and I hurt when I think of her. But if I could choose to have her back, I would say no. I want what's best for her. Being in pain, starving for oxygen is a hard life. I wish she could have stayed longer. I'm glad she is finally healed. I'd like to live my life as well as Hannah lived hers."

—Gary Kingsley, father of Hannah Marie Kingsley (2004–2009)

NOTES

1. Anne Lamott, *Traveling Mercies: Some Thoughts On Faith* (New York: Anchor Books, 1999), 143.
2. Bhagavad Gita, quoted in Subhamoy Das "Healing Words for Tragic Times," http://hinduism.about.com/od/deathdying/a/condolence.htm.
3. The Hebrew Bible, Psalm 23, *The Holy Scriptures According to the Masoretic Text—A New Translation* (Philadelphia: The Lakeside Press, Chicago, 1917), 937.
4. Buddha, quoted in *The Essential Dalai Lama: His Important Teachings*, ed. Rajiv Mehrotra (New York: Penguin Group, Inc., 2005), 122.
5. Laozi, quoted in *Laozi: Quotes & Facts*, ed. Blago Kirov (Longueuil: Osmora, 2014), 16.
6. Abdu'l-Baha, Laura Clifford Barney, and Leslie A. Loveless, *Some Answered Questions* (Wilmette, IL: Baha'i Publishing, 1984), 228.
7. Dalai Lama, *Mind of Clear Light: Advice On Dying And Living a Better Life* (New York: Atria Books, 2003), 39.
8. Martin Luther King Jr., *The Words of Martin Luther King, Jr.*, 2nd ed., ed. Coretta Scott King (New York: New Market Press, 2008), 25.
9. Willa Cather, *Death Comes For the Archbishop* (Sydney: ReadHowYouWant, 2008), 41.

12

A NEW PERSPECTIVE

*"Every day is a miracle. No matter how bad my circumstances,
I have the freedom to choose my attitude to life, even to find joy."*[1]

—Alice Herz-Sommer, Holocaust survivor

CHOOSING THE FUTURE

As the world you know crashes down around you and chaos becomes the norm, the one thing you have control over is your attitude. You basically have two choices:

- You can choose to be bitter and angry.
- You can choose to learn from and accept your new reality.

You have the right to be happy, the right to move on, and the right to be optimistic. Give yourself permission to be more than your present situation. We tend to focus on what has been instead of what can be. You have control over your life's course!

Sometimes there's an identity change after the death of a child. That child no longer calls out your name when they need help or food or love. They no longer call on the telephone. Your connections and conversations are changed. You see their friends much less frequently. Your identity was tied into being that child's parent. When this aspect of your life is turned upside down, you may feel like your identity is unfamiliar to you and that you've lost a part of yourself.

Nikki: *One of the hardest parts of losing a child was feeling as though it* changed who I was inside and out. Once your child is born, you are given a specific role as a parent, protector, teacher, and so on. I was a mother of four. I always counted four heads. I did everything for this child, and after Taylor's death, I felt like I could do nothing for her. I lost who I was. I was not the same person. I felt like my role as a mother was uprooted and personally taken away from me. What was my role? Who was I? What was my identity? What was my new normal?

One morning after Taylor's death I was contemplating my identity and belief system. In doing so, I began to formulate what values and traits were still important to me. I realized I am a mother who loves her children. I believe in life after death and the concept of being resurrected. I am a woman who is human and makes mistakes. I understand that I have limits, and I work to understand the nature of those limits. I then decided what kind of woman I wanted to become. I wrote a description of who I wanted to be on my bathroom mirror. I wrote, "I am a faithful, courageous, quiet mother of four." This helped remind me who I wanted to be, and if I practiced being these things, I could become that person. This is the kind of mother who Taylor would be proud of!

My brother-in-law works with adolescents with self-esteem issues. He gave me a great piece of advice when he told me to go into the bathroom and yell in the mirror: "I am a good mother! I am a good mother!" He said to repeat it until I believed it. It sounds cheesy, but it works. It can be something like, "I am worth something great. God loves me and my child." Or it could be, "I am not perfect, but I am of value." Whatever you need to hear, feel free to say it to yourself. And yelling this phrase might be what you need to do.

— ❧ —

"When writing the story of your life,
don't let anyone else hold the pen."[2]

Harley Davidson advertisement

— ❧ —

Nikki: *Taylor died in July. I decided that on January 1 I was going to become something more than just "the woman who lost her child in a car accident." I hated that label, so I decided to change it. I set a goal for the year and plastered it all over my house so I wouldn't forget it. The phrase I wrote out was,*

TRY THIS
Decide the next chapters of your life. How do you want those chapters to start, and how do you want them to end? Name these chapters and write them down. You can determine your future.

"LOOK BACK WITH GRATITUDE AND FORWARD WITH DETERMINATION!"

This rang true to me on so many levels. I wanted to be grateful for the time I had with Taylor instead of cursing the years I will miss without her. This phrase also helped me to take one step forward when I didn't think I could get out of bed. I looked to the future in a whole new way. I know I've said it before, but I'll say it again. I try to be the mother she would be proud of. Many days I fail, lose my temper, become mad at the world, or forget who I want to be. Then I step back and start again, minute by minute, then hour by hour, then day by day and keep going with determination to improve.

ACCEPTING ACCEPTANCE

An important step in the grief process is the step of acceptance. We have to accept that our child has died. These children may not ever learn to tie their shoes, lose their first tooth, come home from school, get married, buy a home, have children, or grow old on this earth. They will not be present as we enter our twilight years. Acceptance is hard because it is final, but it will also take us to a healthier and more productive place.

Accepting the death of a child may sound wrong and disturbing, but the reality is—it's OK. Without acceptance we tend to rehash our anxieties, over and over again. Acceptance is not forgetting the one you loved but finding joy that they were part of your life.

For some, putting away the child's belongings is a way to find acceptance. Some people leave their child's room exactly how it was when the deceased died. Others pack it up immediately. There is no right or wrong way. The decision is very personal and depends on your feelings and the situation.

Nikki: *Two weeks after the accident, I placed all of Taylor's belongings in newly purchased tubs. I did this because I didn't want anything lost. With three young children under the age of eight, I was terrified that Taylor's things would be lost or misplaced in the chaos of daily life. Alivia didn't even want*

*to go into the bedroom that she had shared
with Taylor because it made her too sad.
So I took photographs of the room, Taylor's
bed, and how the space looked at the time
of death. Will I want these pictures later
on? I don't know, but at least I have them
if I want them. Then I moved the furniture
around and added some new things until
Alivia felt that it was her room now. For
our family, it was important to make this
change to help my children heal.*

TRY THIS
**If your deceased child
could visit you right
now, what would he
or she say to you?
Consider writing
down what your
child would say.**

No one should feel guilty for the
emotions that arise when putting away a
loved one's belongings. Let your emotions flow as you are flooded with
memories. Associations and reminders will come from all of your senses.
You may pick up a shirt or pair of pants and be overwhelmed with memories of the day your child wore that particular piece of clothing. Or you
may smell a piece of clothing and remember what it was like to cuddle
your child.

One sign that you are starting to accept the loss of your child is being
able to reflect on the times you spent with your child as a positive in your
life. Immediately following the loss, these reflections may be too tender.
As time passes, hopefully you will find joy as you remember the good
times together. It helps to write down these memories before they are lost.

WAYS OF ACCEPTING

Another sign that you have achieved a new level of acceptance is when
you find the energy and desire to re-engage in life. There will always be
a place in your heart that misses your child. That child can never be
replaced, but there are ways to begin to fill the emptiness, such as going
to work, taking up a new hobby, getting a pet for companionship, gardening, looking for a job, running or walking, exercising, joining a book club,
meeting friends for lunch, taking a trip, taking a class, or doing volunteer
work.

Nikki: *I began collecting every picture and video of Taylor I could possibly
find. I was like a crazy person, spending many hours into the night organizing
photos and videos into chronological order and saving them onto an external*

hard drive as quickly as possible. It helped me cope.

Find something that helps you to maintain equilibrium emotionally. These activities may not seem important to others, but if they are harmless and bring you happiness, then go for it! Let yourself dive into something new. Give yourself permission to enjoy. It's OK to mentally "check out" for a while as long as you find a healthy balance between "checking out" and recognizing your need to grieve.

Serving others is one way to help heal an aching heart. Acceptance can happen when we begin to reach out to others with similar circumstances. This may be out of our comfort zone, but developing empathy and understanding for those who have experienced loss can benefit not only others but also help in our personal grieving process.

TRY THIS
Take twenty minutes today or tomorrow to write down some of the experiences with your child that you hold dear and don't ever want to forget. Use a simple spiral notebook or your computer or tablet. You may think you will never forget, but memories can fade with time. Write them down.

— ❧ —

"When you find yourself overpowered by melancholy, the best thing to do is go and do something kind for someone."[3]

John Keble

— ❧ —

You may feel guilty at times for focusing on other aspects of life. Remember that finding meaning in your life again does not mean that you are forgetting your child who has died. It's OK to find ways to avoid the pain of grief and to want to smile and laugh again.

THE BEST OF TIMES AND THE WORST OF TIMES

Cammy Wilberger, whose daughter Brooke was kidnapped and murdered, is an example of strength to all. She recalled that she prayed all night the first night when Brooke was missing. As time progressed and Brooke was not located, the grief was unbearable at times. Cammy remembers a day when her body just shut down with grief. She was on the couch and realized that she couldn't even lift her arm. She felt that only God had the power to heal her. The thought came to her that she needed to rise one hour earlier to pray. This meant arising at 4:30 a.m. because she was already getting up at 5:30 to prepare, dress, and drive to her job as an elementary school teacher. During that extra hour she became acutely aware of God's love. She continues to rise an hour early, and she has realized that it's the best hour of her day.

She also keeps a magnet on her refrigerator that says, *"Peace does not mean to be in a place where there is no noise, trouble, or hard work. It means to be in the midst of those things and still be calm in your heart."*

At a speaking engagement in Corvallis, Oregon, Cammy offered these pearls of wisdom to anyone suffering:

- There is still good to be found in this life.
- I miss my daughter dearly, but it's possible to find hope.
- Why wallow in despair when you can live in hope?
- Life is as good as you make it.
- Let's find what we can learn from these trials and put them into action.
- We need to have the hope that we will see our loved ones again.
- We can try to improve our reality instead of trying to escape it.
- Find joy.
- Don't wait for the storm to pass, go dance in the rain.

In moments of reflection, she has asked if, someday, will we look back and wonder if the "worst of times" will actually be viewed as the "best of times" in our lives? She commented that during the "best of times," when we have less conflict or problems, our personal growth is slower. It is actually the times of trials and struggles when we grow and learn. Will we one day be thankful for the "worst of times" and the difference they made in our lives?

— ঝ —

"Adversity is a fact of life. It can't be controlled.
What we can control is how we react to it."

Unknown

— ঝ —

Author Joni Eareckson Tada was an active, athletic teenager when she was involved in a car accident, resulting in her becoming a quadriplegic. She went through the depths of depression and contemplated suicide. She then learned to paint by holding a brush or pencil in her teeth. She went on to sell her artwork, write forty books, record musical albums, star in an autobiographical movie of her life, marry, and become an advocate for people with disabilities. In her book *Joni: An Unforgettable Story*, she wrote some very profound thoughts: "We aren't always responsible for the circumstances in which we find ourselves. However, we are responsible for the way we respond to them. Our lives are like a painting which God is making. Often we jump off the easel, grab a brush, and want to do things ourselves. But when we do this, we only get a bad copy of the masterpiece that He intended for our lives. Your body, in the wheelchair, is only the frame for God's portrait of you. People don't go to an art gallery to admire the picture frames. Their focus is on the quality and character of the painting." Both Cammy Wilberger and Joni Eareckson Tada developed strength through their struggles and disappointments. The way things turned out is often far from what a parent may desire. Many of us yearned for a miracle for our children. We wanted our child to be cured from cancer. We wanted our child's depression to be resolved. We wanted their injuries to be minor and not life-threatening. We wanted our child to be found safe and alive. We wanted to go back in time and remove the death from ever happening. We hoped and prayed for a miracle to happen.

That miracle can happen, but not always in the way for which we hoped and prayed. It is a miracle when a broken bone heals and becomes whole again. It is a miracle when a broken heart heals and becomes whole again. It won't be the same heart. It may be bruised and stretched, but it can be strong again with a steady beat.

— ❧ —

"When one man dies, one chapter is not torn out of the book, but translated into a better language."[4]

John Donne

— ❧ —

You can feel emotionally and spiritually strengthened as a result of struggling through grief and despair. You have dealt with one of the worst tragedies possible and now can cope with anything that may arise in the future. This is the miracle of acceptance and discovering a new perspective.

— ❧ —

"It is your reaction to adversity, NOT the adversity itself that determines how your life's story will develop."[5]

Dieter F. Uchtdorf

— ❧ —

THOUGHTS FROM OTHERS WHO HAVE LOST A CHILD

"Accept the help that is offered, whether it is to help with arrangements for the service, food, babysitting, and so on. You need time to take care of yourself, especially if you have other children. Helping them work through their grief is necessary but may delay you working on your grief. So take a little time and just remember to breathe. Give yourself some slack in all facets of your life. Enjoy the little sweet moments and memories that come. Reflect on the good, and try not to focus on the negative for too long. A way of turning a positive spin on those difficult days is to prepare emotionally by labeling hard days in a positive way. For example: The death date can become his or her heavenly birthday instead of the day they died. The actual anniversary becomes a day of celebrating life instead of focusing on the negative."

—*Brenda Kingsley, mother of Hannah Marie Kingsley (2004–2009)*

"Try not to let yourself dwell on sadness for too long. If it goes on far too long in the black abyss, then it is very difficult to get out of. I would tell myself to cry and let it all out and then I seemed to be able to put the grief aside so that I could function in a normal way.

—*Nadine King, mother of Wendy Nielsen (1960–1961)*

"When we look at tragedy or trials as an opportunity to learn and grow, then it makes it more difficult to hold onto bitterness and loss. We have to choose an explanation of that trial that births the opportunity to make something valuable from it. We have that choice."

—*Greg Merten, father of Scott Fredrick Merten (1973–1990)*

"Talk about your child. Celebrate your child, but not at the expense of any other children in the family. Turn to them and comfort each other. Keep busy. Have projects that you can start and finish. Put your child's things away, but don't give them away. It is a comfort to hug his or her favorite toy and to look at things your child treasured."

—Debora Eichelberger, mother of Dustin Eichelberger (1985–2000)

"I was desperate for a cure and begged God to take me instead of my son. My belief is that I will see him again. Not everyone shares this same belief system, and that is OK with me. I still wish I could hold my son again in his earthly form. If you believe that your children had a purpose while they were here, remember that gift. If you find someone in need of healing, touch their hearts with the one that touched yours."

—Gina Newcomb, mother of Jas Newcomb (1980–2005)

"I had a friend in our church congregation whose adult son died. I felt I should write her a letter, which I did. I addressed some things that had helped me after the death of our baby. I suggested ways that she could find answers to questions, respond to comments, and other things that I had found helpful. When my second daughter died, she sent me a copy of the letter I had sent to her. Another friend suggested I meet her friend to talk about the loss of her son. I had never met this person before. She was willing to meet with me and I was willing to meet with her, so we met for lunch. It was good for both of us to share our different but similar experiences. We still do our yearly lunches. It's a time when we check up on the other to see how we are doing on more than one level."

—Shanna Miller, mother of Lindsay Miller (1978–1978)
and Lynette Miller (1981–2011)

"I've often had other mothers express to me their belief that since I have lost a child, I have this amazing and unparalleled ability to cherish every moment with my other children. I do find that having lived through the loss of one, I live most days with my eyes open wider. Yet when I am standing in a kitchen surrounded by mealtime messes and kids crying and pushing reading logs at me, do I snap and tell them to be quiet? Of course. When my next three babies keep me up for three hours in the middle of the night, do I cry for relief? Absolutely. Then I think of

Elena, and I lean in for one more kiss, stay there for one more cuddle, and pray for one more day in which to do it all again."

—Candida Marie Knight, mother of Elena Marie Knight (2009–2010)

"My perspective on life has changed immensely. I used to try to help people out and be friendly but never do too much. Now I have so much love and empathy for people that are going through a hardship. I want to be there for them—to help them in any single way that I can. I love to bake, so I typically bring treats or dinners over to people or just leave it on their doorsteps. Everyone experiences hardships. You can either let them tear you down, or you can rise above them and reach out to others. Above all, I've learned to love. Love yourself, love everyone, and do all things in love, because that is what it's all about."

—Crystal McNutt, mother of Jackson McNutt (2008–currently dealing with a fatal disease)

NOTES

1. Alice Herz-Sommer, quoted in Caroline Stoessinger *A Century of Wisdom: Lessons from the Life of Alice Herz-Sommer, the World's Oldest Living Holocaust Survivor* (New York: Random House, 2012), 211.

2. Harley Davidson (advertisement), quoted in Gurbaksh Chahal "When You Write the Story of Your Life, Don't Let Anyone Else Hold the Pen," *Huffington Post*, accessed May 20, 2015, http://www.huffingtonpost.com/gurbaksh-chahal/when-you-write-the-story-_b_4951003.html.

3. John Keble, quoted in Rev. George Jackson *The Teaching of Jesus* (New York: A.C. Armstrong and Son, 1903), 185.

4. John Donne in *John Donne: Selections from Divine Poems, Sermons, Devotions, and Prayers*, ed. John E. Booty (Mahwah: Paulist Press, 1990), 271.

5. Dieter F. Uchtdorf, quoted in "General Young Women Meeting: Overcoming adversity key to 'happily ever after,' says President Uchtdorf," *Deseret News*, accessed May 6, 2015, http://www.deseretnews.com/article/700020052/General-Young-Women-Meeting-Overcoming-adversity-key-to-happily-ever-after-says-President.html?pg=all.

13

WAYS TO REMEMBER YOUR CHILD

—

"Death leaves a heartache no one can heal,
love leaves a memory no one can steal." [1]

—From an Irish headstone, Richard Puz, *The Carolinian*

LOVING THROUGH REMEMBERING

When your child dies, you can't imagine *not* remembering their smile, the sound of their voice or laughter, their personality, and the characteristic traits that were unique to them. But as time passes, so can the memories. Preserving them validates that they lived and were loved—it reminds us that they were an integral part of our lives, and it's a way of letting go while still holding onto the relationship.

Many of our most vivid recollections include holidays, gatherings, celebrations, graduations, and birthdays. These events, without your loved one, can be difficult in the grieving process. They are a reminder that things are different. You can fool yourself that your child is simply away at school or on a trip, but when their birthday or a special holiday arrives, you realize that that child should be home and they are not. Talk about your child. Say their name. Share with others your memories. It's normal to want to celebrate their life.

— ❧ —

"People die only when we forget them, my mother explained shortly before she left me. If you can remember me, I will be with you always."[2]

Isabel Allende

— ?< —

WAYS TO REMEMBER

Everybody will remember in different ways. Some parents want to keep the memory of their child alive during certain events, and others may want to kindle that memory on a daily basis. You can remember alone or with family members and friends. You may remember a smell or a laugh, while another family member remembers an event or time shared together. There are different ways to remember. Here are a few ideas:

Before too much time passes, write down memories of your child. Start out slowly, and don't feel overwhelmed. This does not have to be done in one sitting. You can take as much time as you'd like, but the memories will be fresher and fuller if you do them earlier rather than later. None of us want to forget the experiences we had with our child. You will feel more secure in your recollections if you can pick up a journal or notebook and read over the memories. You can write about his or her favorite foods, friends, music, activities, sports, classes, and colors. You can recall what made them happy or what made them sad. You might want to write about some personal interactions or experiences you had with that child: the birth, an illness, or a school project. Look at photos and write down the story behind some of your favorites. We usually don't take photos unless it's

TRY THIS
Save some of your child's clothing or bedding. Be careful of well-meaning family members who come to help clean out your child's clothing and belongings. Simply put those items in a box that you have chosen to keep. Later, when you have the time and energy, you may want to make or hire someone to create a "comfort quilt" out of the material from these items. When you're missing that child, simply wrap yourself in your quilt, and you will be reminded of happier times from the past.

something we want to remember. Ask others to share their memories with you also.

Keep a portrait of the child in your home. Just because your child has died, you don't need to put away photos of that child. It may be painful initially to see their framed picture on the mantle or bookshelf, but it will probably bring comfort to you and to other family members later on. Siblings need to know that you remember that their brother or sister lived. If you remove any sign of their deceased brother or sister from the home, it may confuse them about what is important to you. If you have other children, you may want to consider giving a picture of your deceased child to each of them to keep in their bedrooms or homes.

Remember the conversations you had with your child. Think back on moments when you smiled or laughed or cried together.

Take all the photos of your child and scan them into the computer. If they are already on the computer, be sure and back these photos onto a hard drive or online. If your computer crashes, you don't want to lose these precious visual remembrances.

Create a shadow box to hang in your home. Choose one or more objects that evoke a special memory of that child. It might be something like a pair of shoes from his or her childhood, a handwritten letter, a beloved toy, a graduation photo and diploma, or a bunch of their favorite phrases.

On your child's birthday, celebrate his or her life by looking at photos or videos of the child. Plan a meal around his or her favorite foods, and engage in your child's favorite games or activities. Verbally share memories of the child.

Plant a memory garden to honor your child. Each year, on his or her birthday, add a new plant or tree. Let other family members help make selections for the garden.

Give monetary donations made in the memory of your child to a specific nonprofit or other worthy organization. The name of this organization can be written in the obituary or in the program at a memorial service. Many friends and family members want to know what to do to ease the pain. They want to let you know that they won't forget your child, and they appreciate knowing a way that you have chosen in which to remember your child. If you can't think of an organization to serve as a recipient, you can simply use the wording, "Memorial donations may be made to an organization or nonprofit of your choice."

— 🌿 —

Those we love don't go away, they walk beside us every day, unseen,
unheard but always near, still loved, still missed and very dear.

Unknown

— 🌿 —

Alice: *We chose the Ronald McDonald House in Portland, Oregon, as
the recipient of memorial gifts for our daughter Lora. We had spent many
nights at this wonderful home away from home with Lora during her cancer
treatments. We were so thankful for this refuge in the storm—a place that
provided a haven for our entire family when needed. It felt good to know
that donations made in her name would benefit other families like ours who
had to travel to Portland for their child's various treatments and surgeries.
Friends came up with their own memorial gifts, and that touched our hearts.
One friend paid for a new library book that included a label stating that this
was purchased in memory of Lora Dorothea Rampton. Neighbors pitched in
and bought a beautiful dogwood tree in Lora's memory. The local DeMoss-
Durdan Funeral Home covered the cost of her casket. These gifts from friends
and family brought happiness to our hearts. They helped us know that she had
made a difference with her short life on earth and that she was remembered.*

Nikki: *During the Christmas season, we wrote down on slips of paper all the
nice things that we saw members of our family do for one another. We put
these slips of paper in Taylor's stocking. Before opening the gifts on Christmas
morning, we read aloud all of these things that seemed to emphasize the true
meaning of Christmas.*

Alice: *Each year, when we cut down or buy our Christmas tree, we save
some of the boughs. We take these and gather them together in a simple
arrangement with a red bow. During the holidays, we place these boughs
on Lora's grave. It's our way of sharing our Christmas tree and celebrations
with her. We gather in a circle at her grave and sing the Christmas carol
"Silent Night." The last refrain of that song has special meaning, "Sleep in
heavenly peace." We always hang up the stocking with Lora's name. At the
end of the season, we find little trinkets and gifts that the other children had
placed in her stocking.*

*On the anniversary of her first birthday following her death, we wanted
to do something special. As a family, we decided to go to a circus. We thought*

that it was something that Lora would've enjoyed also. It turned out to be a bad idea! We sat behind the smelly animal cages. We didn't like seeing the animals whipped as they came into the arena. No one had any fun, and we left early. Upon our arrival at home, we pulled out videos of Lora to watch. Together, we just laughed and cried. It was much better than the circus. Be prepared that not every idea or event you plan to memorialize your child is going to work out. Give it another chance.

When a child dies, a parent doesn't know what to do or what steps to take next. Doing something to memorialize your child will give you a purpose and may bring you a sense of peace. It also helps friends and family know of a specific way to support you. The various ways we remember our children confirms that they will always be a part of our lives.

— ⚜ —

"I answer the heroic question, 'Death, where is thy sting?' with 'It is in my heart and mind and memories.'"[3]

Maya Angelou

— ⚜ —

THOUGHTS FROM OTHERS WHO HAVE LOST A CHILD

"Make known that you want to be an organ or blood donor. This can usually be designated on your driver's license. Our daughter gave the gift of life through organ donation and saved the life of a single dad with five children. Hannah is a hero."

—*Brenda Kingsley, mother of Hannah Marie Kingsley (2004–2009)*

"Designate memorial donations to something that is meaningful to you or to your child. There are many wonderful community agencies that could use financial help, and friends and family want to do something that will make a difference. Our friends and family donated to the Cystic Fibrosis Foundation in Jas's name. Some of them still contribute each year."

—*Gina Newcomb, mother of Jas Newcomb (1980–2005)*

"We set up a memorial fund and designated the money to support the Oregon Shakespeare Festival. We had a chair in one of the theatres dedicated to Sam and added quotes from *Hamlet*, which was his favorite play. The remainder of the funds went to support a suicide prevention organization that one of Sam's friends had been involved with."

—*Ann and Mike Lahr, parents of Sam Lahr (1989–2009)*

"Dustin, my son, was killed as he was in a crosswalk on a major highway in our town. After his death, I spent six years working with the office of a US senator, state officials, and city officials to install a pedestrian signal, improve the crosswalk, and lower the highway speed. I involved newspapers, TV stations, local businesses, and school officials. Many of the local people stepped up to write letters, sign petitions, donate food for meetings, and so on to support this project. There is now a much-improved crosswalk. The speed limit was lowered. A pedestrian crossing light has been installed. All this was done to prevent another child loss and as a way to honor our son."

—*Debora Eichelberger, mother of Dustin Guy Eichelberger (1985–2000)*

"We remember our son Craig by talking to each other about him. We remember what he did and said. Family members constantly recall our good times together during his childhood, youth, and adulthood. We have photos of the family posted around our home. We visit his grave often and stay in close touch with his widow and their children."

—*Nancy and Craig Leman, parents of Craig A. Leman (1956–1998)*

"We have always had the pencil drawing of him on the wall that a friend did for his funeral announcements. Next to the drawing is a statement in calligraphy about how this life and the next intertwine. We still talk about him. Our daughter Anjai recently created a scrapbook about Dallan. Now she is working on a photo book of his life. She is planning on giving a copy to each family member so that his siblings and the next generation will always have this book to remember Dallan. I keep his coat in my closet. It is the last one he had, and I have many memories of him wearing it. It symbolizes that he is part of my life and will never be forgotten. When I see his coat, I am reminded again of how he is part of me and how much I love him."

—*Susan Fisher, mother of Dallan Fisher (1988–1992)*

"As the first anniversary of Hannah's death was coming upon us, I decided that I didn't want that day to always be a day of sadness. I knew that my youngest child, who was two and a half at the time, wouldn't understand what the day was, and I didn't want that to be a day every year that the rest of my kids were sad and dreading. I decided that August 28 was Hannah's "heavenly" birthday. I believe what the Bible says that when a saint comes home, all heaven rejoices. On that day we take Hannah's favorite-colored balloons out to the cemetery; we write something on the balloons and then let them go. Then we go do something nice for the hospital staff that took such good care of Hannah over her short life. We bring a basket of muffins, bread, cookies, and so on, with a card thanking them for caring for others."

—*Brenda Kingsley, mother of Hannah Marie Kingsley (2004–2009)*

"Right before Hannah's birthday, we go shopping and buy a bunch of items to make up Samaritan Purse boxes. Then on Hannah's birthday we have friends over who also bring items, and we all put the boxes together. The next day we bring them to the drop-off location. My thought is this: Hannah was happy and excited on her birthday. Why not bless someone else that day and bring a smile to his or her face? Hannah would like that. At Christmas we buy gifts for names on the local Angel Tree. We take a picture of the gift with the name tag and put it in Hannah's stocking. We set a dollar amount, and each member of our family gets to pick a place that they would like to donate to in Hannah's name. We put a copy of the check or a picture of the place we are donating to and put that in the stocking. Then on Christmas, we talk about why we wanted to give to that person or place."

—*Brenda Kingsley, mother of Hannah Marie Kingsley (2004–2009)*

"Jas would talk to some of the other patients about cystic fibrosis (CF) at the request of the nurses at Oregon Health Sciences University (OHSU). He was compassionate and could explain the questions in a way only the two of them could understand. No matter the age of the person, he had a unique way of touching them. When he was seventeen years old, the nurses asked him to speak to a twenty-five-year-old young lady staying at OHSU while he was there who also had CF. I was amazed and deeply moved by his compassion and straightforward language. She seemed taken aback by his lack of restraint; she cried, and he hugged her and then told her to buck up! They both laughed, and she was discharged that day. I don't know her circumstances, but I believe Jas made an impact on her heart. I still hear from people all over about how Jas touched their lives in some way. That is memorial enough."

—*Gina Newcomb, mother of Jas Newcomb (1980–2005)*

"I think to live well and be an inspirational example is the best tribute to my son Lane. Lane's grave marker has his picture on it. It also has carved into the stone a boy skiing and playing soccer. The one of him playing soccer was a duplication of a picture taken of him. Also, my first grandchild's name is Riley Lane, and one of my nephews named his daughter Delaney in honor of Lane. They call her Laney."

—*Karen Martin, mother of Lane Anthony Martin (1971–1982)*

"Every member of the family has a silver band that we wear on a finger. Inside it has that person's nickname for Hannah or a favorite saying about her inscribed. It is something that is special to us. It's a simple reminder of her and that one day we will see our special girl again."

—*Brenda Kingsley, mother of Hannah Marie Kingsley (2004–2009)*

"Plant a tree or plant to commemorate the life of your child. One aunt bought a tree to plant in our yard in memory of Marc, and it meant a lot to all of us."

—*Janet and Brent Harris, parents of Marc David Harris (1980–1986)*

"We started Cameron's Fight Big Bags to help families in crisis at the hospital with the basics until their families can get there to help them cope. Blood drives were held in his honor. We donated his unopened Christmas presents to the ICU and the Pediatric Cancer Unit. We planted a tree where he liked to play and mixed the dried flowers from his funeral into our flower beds. Maybe they will have seeds that grow. We sent thank-you cards with Cameron's picture to all the people who have helped along the way."

—*Shelley Merrill, mother of Cameron Merrill (2010–2013)*

"Lynette's thirtieth birthday was just a little over two months after her death, and my daughter and I thought of a way to celebrate. We called it LAFF Fest. L stands for *laughter,* A for *arts,* F for *film,* and the other F for *food.* Using social media, we invited anyone who knew her to celebrate her birthday by doing some activity that they would've done with Lynette that related to LAFF. We asked them to post their activities on Lynette's or my Facebook page. It was wonderful to read those comments and to participate in our own LAFF Fest activities. We have continued to do this since her death. I also wore one of Lynette's necklaces for the first six months after her death. When she died I bought a yellow bracelet for her to be buried with and a matching one for me to wear. I also bought the same bracelets for her grandmother and some of her closest friends. About nine months after Lynette's death, I held a lunch for some of Lynette's closest friends. I had made them each a memory book with some of Lynette's favorite recipes (she loved to cook), which were also part of the luncheon menu. I put some pictures of Lynette in the book with the recipes. After lunch they looked through the box of pictures that Lynette had saved, and I let them pick some out to add to their books. These women also helped me sort through that box of pictures, reacquainting me with known friends of Lynette and identifying others unknown to me. They gave me the courage to save some representative pictures and get rid of the rest. There was laughter, tears, and healing."

—*Shanna Miller, mother of Lindsay Miller (1978–1978)*
and Lynette Miller (1981–2011)

"We chose scholarships for young adults in Ukraine as one of the recipients of a memorial gift in Josh's name. We also designated Doernbecher Children's Hospital in Portland as beneficiary of memorial donations."

—*Beth Nelson, mother of Joshua Roland Nelson (1992–2012)*

"One of the grief books I read had a section on grandparents and their grief. I read it to better understand that I'm not the only one who feels a loss about Emma's death. In the book, it mentions that creating something for the one lost can help in the grieving process. I asked my mother and mother-in-law if they wanted to make something in Emma's memory. My mother wrote a "from the heart" poem, and my mother-in-law did a beautifully symbolic painting. I plan on putting them both up on the wall next to a picture of Christ holding a baby, which was given to us by my husband's aunt and uncle. These things are special to me and remind me how much Emma was loved and that she is still loved and missed."

—*Caitlin Bradshaw, mother of Emma Joy Bradshaw (2013–2013)*

"Troy played the trumpet, trombone, and tuba during the time he was in high school and college. The tuba he played belonged to the school, but the trumpet and trombone were among his possessions. Neither of his sons were interested in playing the instruments, so I took them to be evaluated, and only the trumpet was worth cleaning and repairing. After it was fixed, I took the trumpet to Corvallis High School, where Troy loved playing in the band, the pep band, and the Blue Tones (a jazz group). I gave the trumpet to the band director. I thought I could do it without breaking down, but I couldn't. Still, it makes me happy to know that it's there. The band director told me that they used instruments such as this for special occasions."

—*Judy Juntunen, mother of Troy Juntunen (1967–2012)*

"At Christmas, we donate the amount we may have spent on gifts for Hannah to various charities. Usually the kids pick how we donate the money. This year, we had a friend of my son's stay with us who had no family around, so we bought gifts for him. On her birthday, we all take the day off work and school. We go out to breakfast. We go to a local bread store and buy the biggest basket they have and fill it with cinnamon rolls, cookies, and treats. Then we take the basket to the hospital and give it to the nurses. We include a note thanking them for all they do and a picture of Hannah. Many of our traditions are from our friends. My friend Tom writes letters to his daughter who has passed away and puts them in her stocking at Christmas. We still hang up a stocking for Hannah. We release balloons at the gravesite (this was an idea from Tom). The kids also write messages to Hannah on the balloons, and then we let them go. Our traditions have changed with time. That has been important, because we are changing and our grief is changing. We don't want it to be an empty tradition. We talk about what we want to do each year. Memorializing is for us, and so it should be special for us. Hannah doesn't need it; she has everything she could ever want in heaven."

—*Gary Kingsley, father of Hannah Marie Kingsley (2004–2009)*

"In December 2014, as family and friends, we installed a bench in Alex's honor that was placed in McDonald Forest outside of Corvallis, Oregon. The bench was made from a tree that had fallen in the forest earlier that year. Alex grew up running the trails in this forest, and the bench is on one of his well-worn trails. We spread some of his ashes under the bench and extended an invitation to anyone to find the bench, take a moment to relax, breathe deeply, and find gratitude in your life."

—*Pat Newport, mother of Alex Newport-Berra (1981–2014)*

"I have pictures of Elena in several places in our home. I have one spot just for baby Elena, our forever baby. I also include her with pictures of our other girls. She will always be a part of our family, and I love to be surrounded by her. I also love that all my daughters, even those who came after her, recognize her in pictures, because in a way, they still know her because I've kept her alive in our home."

—*Candida Marie Knight, mother of Elena Marie Knight (2009–2010)*

NOTES

1. Richard Puz, quoted in Joshua Mendrala *Gifted* (Raleigh: Lulu, 2014), 275.
2. Isabel Allende, *Eva Luna* (New York: Dial Press, 2005), 43.
3. Maya Angelou, quoted in Terri O'Neill "The heartbreaking cry of pain," *Patch*, accessed May 22, 2015, http://patch.com/illinois/lemont/heartbreaking-cry-pain-0.

14

FRIENDS AND FAMILY

How to Help

"God does notice us and he watches over us. But it is usually through another person that he meets our needs." [1]

—Spencer W. Kimball

FRIENDS AND FAMILY

What can *you* do for those suffering? First and foremost, don't ignore the fact that a death has happened. Don't pretend it didn't happen and that everything is just fine. Acknowledge the fact that you know they have experienced a great loss and that you are very sorry. Next, respond to their needs. Don't ask, just do. Anticipate a friend's needs, not your own, but also respect their space and privacy. Know the person you want to serve. What were they like before the death of their child? Walk in their shoes. Serve them, not yourself.

TO DO IMMEDIATELY

"I'm so sorry."

Immediately following the death of a child, this is all you need to say. There is no perfect phrase to ease the pain, but heartfelt sympathy and a hug is sometimes all that's needed to show your condolences. Then help! There are myriad details to be taken care of after a child dies, and often the parents are in shock—dazed and in a heavy fog. They may not even *know* what their needs are. Create a list of specific things that might need to be done, and ask them which of these things they would like you (or others) to do. Here are some suggestions:

- With their permission, make phone calls to family and friends to inform them of the death. This can be very difficult for a grieving parent to do over and over again.
- Pick up family or friends from airports, train stations, and so on who may be coming from out of town.
- Create a program for the memorial service that can be given out to those who attend.
- Obtain a guest book or make one. Encourage those who come to the service to sign in. Later, the parents will appreciate the reminder of who attended.
- Provide flowers for the casket or tables at the service.
- Take photos of the memorial service and graveside service.
- Make a recording of the service.
- Create a video of the child's life.
- Compile a collage of the child's photos.
- Help select clothing if the child is to be buried.
- Help clean the house.
- Ask if you can wash, iron, dry clean, or repair any clothing that family members are planning to wear to the service.
- Wash the car.
- Mow the lawn.
- Stay at the family's home while they're at the service. There have been rare cases when homes have been burglarized during a memorial service by someone who checked the time of the service in an obituary notice.
- Provide food for family and guests.
- Provide a gift certificate to a restaurant to cover the cost of a meal for the family so they don't have to worry about meal preparation or clean up for one evening.

WAYS TO HELP ON AN ONGOING BASIS

In the weeks, months, and years following the death, you can continue supporting and helping the family that's lost an important person. Their pain may never heal, so your support will be appreciated for the long haul!

Nikki: *A good friend of mine always seemed to show up at my doorstep at just the right time. She just showed up to give me a hug one day. Having a friend* *who stopped by to remind me that she was there for me was so appreciated. She seemed like an angel who was there when I needed her.*

Ask yourself what this person would normally be doing or appreciate if they were not going through this most difficult situation of having lost a child. For example, if they are normally a clean and tidy homeowner, then they may appreciate an offer to help clean their house. If they are usually low on cash, write them a check, or better yet, give them an envelope with cash. If they bake often, bring them the homemade bread that they would have normally baked that day. If Friday is their usual "pizza for dinner" night, bring over a pizza on Friday. If it's the end of the month and they are usually punctual with their bills, ask if they need your help in making the due date. With permission, take a peek in their fridge. Buy the milk and eggs if they need it. These simple acts of kindness can go a long way.

MORE IDEAS . . .

- If there are other children in the family, consider dropping them off and picking them up from school, driving them to practices and games and other appointments, watching them, helping with their homework, giving them love and attention, and so on.
- Help with home administrative tasks—insurance forms, bills, scheduling appointments.
- Offer to do the grocery shopping. Offer to do it the next time too.
- Encourage your friend or family member to attend a support group meeting and perhaps go with them.
- Participate in an activity your friend or family member typically enjoys doing, for example: taking a walk, going to a movie, playing a specific game.
- Make a quilt from clothing or bedding used by the child.
- Write down memories and gather photos of the child for the parents.
- Remember the deceased child's birth date and death date. A phone call, email, text, or card letting them know that you remember that day is a simple but important gesture of kindness.

If they reject your offers, lists, or gifts of time and money, don't take it personally. Let your friend have the upper hand. Rejection may be their only way of having a sense of control in their "out of control" life.

Nikki: *I love my family and friends, but it got to a point where I thought they wouldn't want to be around me because I was depressing. I heard myself on numerous occasions apologizing for "being a downer."*

I continued to do this until I was chastized by a dear friend of mine. The conversation went as such: "I'm sorry I keep talking about this. I must be so depressing to be around."

My friend replied, "What on earth are you saying? I wouldn't be here with you if I didn't care. If something good was happening in your life, I would want to hear about that too. Plus, don't deprive me of helping you get through this. I like to be helpful." Well, that is what I needed to hear. I then stopped apologizing so much and enjoyed having people around me who were OK with just listening. I later learned that my close family and friends wanted to hear from me, read my blog, and check my Facebook posts because they wanted to understand how I was dealing with my loss.

My dear friend knew what a struggle it was going to be on the first birthday of my little girl after her death. So she sent out an invite to all my closest friends to tape record their own family message saying, "Happy Birthday, Taylor," while releasing balloons into the sky. These families then sent their tapes to my friend for editing. She combined them into one glorious gift for me and my family. It meant so much to me. It made me feel like my entire community was celebrating her birthday and life with us on that special day.

The sweetest, most meaningful thing my dear friends did for me was on the one-year anniversary of my daughter's death (her heavenly birthday). They knew I was going to go to the grave site that day, so unbeknownst to me, they sent out emails to many mutual friends and acquaintances. Long story short, when my family arrived at Taylor's grave site, there was a huge array of flowers, gifts, toys for my other children, windwheels, balloons, and so on. It covered more than the entire grave site and absolutely blew us away. There was also a beautiful box that was full of cards with people expressing their love for our family. All in all, we were so touched. It turned a tough day into a really good memory.

TRY THIS
One year after the death of your friend's child, send a note with your memories of that child. Let your friend know that you have not forgotten your friend or his or her child.

Alice: *Every year, around Lora's death date, I have an older friend call to tell me she remembers Lora and is thinking of me and my family. She has lost two of her four children and understands loss. Her calls are always a comfort and a reminder to me that there are people out there who still remember Lora, even decades later.*

Simple gestures of support make all the difference immediately following the death, or years later.

LISTENING

Your friend or family member's burden can be made lighter by a good listener. And that listener can be you! This isn't always a simple task. It means really listening without judgment, advice, impatience, or minimizing the loss. Rather, let the parent talk as long as he or she needs. One fear of parents is that their child will be forgotten. Letting them talk about him or her is a form of remembering. This is not a time to tell your story or share your loss. It's a time to listen to their story and focus on what they are experiencing.

Listening may also mean simply sitting in silence if that's what they would prefer.

Grieving parents don't necessarily want someone to fix things. If they did, they would want you to bring their child back. Author Curtis Thompson says, "To listen freely without thought of time, place, or constraint is still the most appreciated gift a person can give. It is important for the griever to be able to talk and reminisce about the lost loved one or even the incident."[2]

A death of a child can make parents angry. They may look for someone to blame. You may discover that their anger is being projected onto you even though it may not make sense to you. Inward blame for the parent may be more than they can manage at the time. Experiences like this can test relationships.

WHAT TO WATCH FOR

Sometimes grieving can spiral into a more serious problem like clinical depression. As you support your friend or family member, watch for signs that he or she may need to see a doctor for help. Some symptoms to watch for include the following:

- insomnia
- severe fatigue
- sleeping all day
- extreme self-criticism, bitterness, guilt, or anger
- sudden weight loss or gain
- withdrawal from everyday activities and social engagements
- difficulty functioning in daily life
- unusual focus on the death
- neglecting personal hygiene
- alcohol or drug abuse
- continued inability to enjoy life
- hallucinations
- extreme feelings of hopelessness
- talking about suicide

If you begin to see these symptoms on a regular basis, share with them an "I" message such as "I am worried about you" or "I love you, and I'm scared." Encourage them to seek professional help. In a downward spiral, individuals may not even be aware of a change in their emotional, physical, or mental health. Author Letty Cottin Pogrebin shares three suggestions on how to be a friend to someone going through any type of a difficult situation:[3]

1. Tell me what's helpful and what's not.
2. Tell me if you want to be alone and when you want company.
3. Tell me what to bring and when to leave. You set the tone: this is our policy, to be truthful with each other.

Cottin Pogrebin's three points can apply to relationships among friends when one has lost a child also. The death of a child can be burdening, but thoughtful friends and caring family members can definitely lighten that burden. Sometimes they just need a little encouragement and direction to help in a meaningful way.

— ❧ —

A good friend is . . . a safety bar on your emotional roller coaster, a therapist without the high hourly fee, a nonprescription mood enhancer.

Unknown

— ❧ —

A caring and concerned family member or friend will try to anticipate the needs of a grieving person. They will reach out in appropriate
ways to offer support and love.

THOUGHTS FROM OTHERS WHO HAVE LOST A CHILD:

"Sam's best friend and wife named their baby after Sam. His cousins
had a star named for Sam. Linn Benton Community College, where Sam
attended, purchased a Shakespeare book for the college library and placed
a memorial bookplate in the book in his memory. We had a lot of people
step in and make the memorial service happen, including the slide presentation, guest book, food, printing of the programs, and so on."

—Ann Lahr, mother of Sam Lahr (1989–2009)

"It meant a lot when people just said they were sorry about his death
or shared memories they had of him. We appreciated when friends came
by with food, a card, or a book or just to say sorry and to give a hug. We
liked receiving photos of Joshua that a friend had taken. It is much more
helpful for a person to ask 'Can we go on a walk together (or out to lunch
or another suggestion) on Monday or Tuesday?' rather than 'I'd love to go
for a walk (or lunch or another suggestion) with you. Give me a call when
you would like to.' I want to do things with people, but it takes energy
and getting past inertia to set things up. By having them make a specific
offer, I can accept what works rather than trying to call and figure out
details. It has been nice to have people call and have them send emails,
notes in the mail, or texts to check in even now (four months after his
death), saying things like, 'Thinking of you.'"

—Beth Nelson, mother of Joshua Roland Nelson (1992–2012)

"The people who care about Craig mention him affectionately, such as
school friends and family members who often recall our times with him."

—Nancy Leman, mother of Craig A. Leman (1956–1998)

"Our friends were such a huge help that we couldn't have made
Hannah's service as nice as it was without them. Meals were set up for us
during that time, which was really nice. There were money, flowers, and
donation of time to help with the cost of the service. Donations were also
made in memory of Hannah to Ronald McDonald House in Portland,

Oregon; Mended Little Hearts of Anchorage and Haitian Christian Mission. Some of the most helpful things that people said were simply, 'I'm sorry,' 'I'm here for you,' and 'I'll be praying for you.' There really isn't anything a person can say that's going to make you feel better."

—*Brenda Kingsley, mother of Hannah Marie Kingsley (2004–2009)*

"People who had lost a child wrote from many places and shared their experience. Another thing that was helpful was the support that came from friends and family during the whole first year and longer. These good people just loved us. We felt they really cared."

—*Janet Harris, mother of Marc David Harris (1980–1986)*

"There were donations made in Dustin's name to nonprofit organizations. The amount of flowers sent to the service was overwhelming. The best and most thoughtful of the flowers was the live rose bush that was given from the middle school faculty. The bush continues to grow and produce blossoms thirteen years later. Also, it was important to our family that Dustin be buried in a full scout uniform, so the community made that happen by picking up all the merit badges we needed and the extra clothing to complete the uniform."

—*Debora Eichelberger, mother of Dustin Guy Eichelberger (1985–2000)*

"My brother and his wife came from another state to be with us on Lane's first death anniversary. Another friend who wasn't even around at the time of Lane's death, nor had he known him well, began to call or send a card on Lane's death anniversary each year. A couple that owned a book store wouldn't allow us to pay them for the programs that were printed and handed out at the funeral. . . . Another young couple moved to our state after Lane's death. Although they had never met Lane, they called or sent a card on his death anniversary each year. They did not have children of their own, but they always were sensitive to include our oldest son, Shawn, in any activities we spent together."

—*Karen Martin, mother of Lane Anthony Martin (1971–1982)*

"Sometimes an emergency or illness brings you to the hospital without time for preparation. Items that are nice for families and individuals to receive during this time are Starbucks gift cards, toys for your child, treats, pajamas, flip flops, cash, tissues, mascara, and so on. Friends helped us in many ways by making donations in his honor to organizations that help kids, organizing or participating in fun runs in his honor, purchasing candles in his honor at cancer runs, purchasing flowers and a tree and bird bath, sharing stories of how they appreciate their kids more, hugging their children more often, helping their children pray more, talking to God more, and becoming closer to God. I really loved to hear that Cameron had changed someone's life significantly."

—*Shelley Merrill, mother of Cameron Merrill (2010–2013)*

"My husband was a few weeks from graduating in an MBA program. The whole school put together a donation fund and also put together a binder with personal notes. Independently, families from the program dropped off meals, treats, flowers, and notes. One friend even brought us a stroller. I had just shared how excited I was to buy a particular double jogging stroller for my two daughters. When she heard that my baby had died, she thought of the empty seat in that new stroller. So she went out and bought me the same stroller in a single child model. Another woman came and offered to do my laundry to spare me the pain of having to wash baby clothes that I wouldn't dress Elena in again."

—*Candida Marie Knight, mother of Elena Marie Knight (2009–2010)*

"We were pleased when friends gave us a tree to plant in Lynette's memory with a note describing why they had picked that tree and the symbolism they attached to it regarding our daughter."

—*Shanna Miller, mother of Lindsay Miller (1978–1978)*
and Lynette Miller (1981–2011)

"One of my friends made small cards (2 × 3 inches) with Alex's photo, birth, and death dates, one of his original quotes on the front, and an original poem and link to his website on the back. I will always use these to give to people who truly want to know more about Alex."

—*Pat Newport, mother of Alex Newport-Berra (1981–2014)*

"One of the most helpful things was when people didn't try to stay away because they didn't know what to say. A simple 'I am sorry this had to happen' was enough."

—Susan Fisher, mother of Dallan Fisher (1988–1992)

"While I appreciated all the cards we received, I especially valued the ones that added a note about something they remembered about Troy. Since that time, when I write a sympathy note to someone, and I knew the person who died well enough, I try to add more in my note to the family than 'you are in our thoughts and prayers.' Shortly after Troy's death, one of his friends in Richland started a group on Facebook entitled 'Remembering Troy.' It was so wonderful to read the posts and see the ways that Troy had touched so many lives in positive ways. Friends posted how he had helped and inspired them in a recovery group to which he belonged. Others mentioned how he had touched not only their lives but also their children's at school or Sunday School."

—Judy Juntunen, mother of Troy Juntunen (1967–2012)

"We felt a huge outpouring of love from friends and family. There were more meals than we could have ever eaten. Women came over and cleaned our house. They offered to host out-of-town visitors who were coming for the funeral. I loved it when people wanted to talk about Megan. Some people didn't know what to say. I just appreciated it when people would remember her in some way in their conversation."

—Elaine Forrest, mother of Megan Forrest (1985–2005)

NOTES

1. Spencer W. Kimball, "Small Acts of Service," accessed May 6, 2015, https://www.lds.org/ensign/1974/12/small-acts-of-service?lang=eng.
2. Curtis Thompson, "What Should I Say?—What Should I Do?" LDSMissionaryMoms.com, accessed May 6, 2015, http://www.ldsmissionary-moms.com/helptopics/About_Grieving_and_Giving_Solace/#What_Should_I_Say_-_What_Should_I_Do.
3. Letty Cottin Pogrebin, *How to Be a Friend to a Friend Who's Sick* (New York: Public Affairs, 2013), 33.

— ❦ —

THE CHILDREN WHO
INSPIRE US

These are the children who are the inspiration behind this book. They
changed our lives, and this is one way we honor them.

Taylor Michelle King
March 23, 2011–July 27, 2012

Taylor had the blondest hair and bluest eyes and brought a smile to everyone she met. She loved her older brother, Tyson, and older sisters, Natalie and Alivia. She wanted to be big like her siblings. She always slept with her head on her mattress and her bottom in the air. Taylor loved to dance and play in the shower.

She died in a tragic car accident after a short sixteen-month sojourn here on earth.

Now we live for you and think of you daily. You will be sorely missed. We love you, Taylor. There is no foot too small that it cannot leave an imprint on this world.

Lora Dorothea Rampton
May 5, 1984–January 9, 1986

Lora was full of life. She loved to dance with her Grandpa Bob and climb into kitchen drawers. Her favorite foods were fresh black-berries and clam chowder. She was full of fun, curiosity, and mischievousness and loved to play with her brothers and sisters.

At the time of her birth, she had five older siblings: Lisa, Meta, Marcus, Anna, and Sara. Her younger brother, Bobby, was born a year and one day after Lora's death date.

She was diagnosed with neuroblastoma at fourteen months. Chemotherapy, intraoperative radiation, surgeries, and holistic methods could not stop the cancer.

She brightened the lives of everyone she met and taught her family about the ties that bind.

"So tiny, so small, so loved by all."

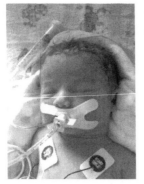

Emma Joy Bradshaw
August 14th, 2013–August 14, 2013

Emma Joy was beautiful with a full head of dark hair just like the hair color of her mama and big sister, Jane. We treasure the short time we got to hold her little hands and kiss her sweet, round cheeks.

She passed away peacefully in the arms of her parents, Richard and Caitlin Bradshaw, as we whispered to her words of love and hope. She brought us all so much joy from the moment we found out we were pregnant.

We all love her and miss her dearly and dream of the day we will meet again.

Jason Alan Newcomb
October 28, 1980–September 25, 2005

Jason ("Jas") lost his battle with cystic fibrosis one month before his twenty-fifth birthday. Jas was a radiance of comedy and determination that touched the hearts and minds of so many people in his time here with us. His quick-witted humor, contagious laughter, and mischievous smile were like magnets.

Always in a rush to conquer the milestones of everyday life, he would never allow his illness to hold him back or allow anyone to treat him as a frail individual. He had the ability to look into the heart of acquaintances, friends, and loved ones and speak the words of encouragement and love that they needed to hear.

The biblical meaning of the name Jason is "he that cures" or "a healing." Since we had no idea if his illness at the time we chose his name, I certainly wanted this to be a sign from God that he would be healed. Little did we know that his name, his person, and his presence would be so impactful to so many people, giving true meaning to the name he was given at birth. His gravestone reads, "Gift of God."

Wendy Lynne Nielsen
July 12, 1960–December 4, 1961

Wendy was enthusiastically welcomed by her parents and three brothers (Chase, Scott, and Greg). She had short light-brown hair, which became more blonde as she played in the sunshine of Western Samoa, where our family moved when she was eleven months old.

She brought volumes of sweetness, love, and happiness to our family, and she loved playing outside with her brothers, especially in the warm rains of Samoa.

Wendy was tragically and fatally run over in the driveway of the family home in Pesega, Upolu, Western Samoa, two days after the birth of her brother Chad. Our family was later blessed with four more boys (Cary, Thor, Shawn, and Joel). Wendy was and is our little angel.

Dustin Guy Eichelberger
August 19, 1985–July 7, 2000

Dustin was a kind-hearted soul and was known for seeking out friends and family who were sad and needed cheering up. His greatest enjoyment was scouting.

He had completed his eighth year of schooling and was looking forward to being in high school. Dustin was killed just before his fifteen birthday when he was struck by a car while walking in a crosswalk.

He has two brothers (Ryan and Cory) and three sisters (Cindy, Nicole, and Jennifer).

"How great shall be your joy."

Craig Averill Leman
March 2, 1956–July 8, 1998

Craig was treasured by family and friends for his intelligence, courage, generosity, affection and for his unique talent at entertaining repartee and storytelling. His hobbies included archery, photography, iris gardening, gem polishing, and golf. A voracious reader, Craig possessed an extraordinary knowledge of history. He was a terrific father to his two sons, Craig F. and Eric. We laughed often in his presence.

Craig and his wife, Janet, worked and lived in Washington, DC; Philadelphia; Tokyo; and the New York and San Francisco areas. He earned a master's degree from the Wharton School of Business and worked in the securities industry, always finding time to make new friends. His frequent business trips often included a visit to the local art museum.

When Craig was diagnosed with cancer, he and Janet brought their young sons back to the Corvallis area. Craig was eager to spend his remaining time with family and wanted to give Janet and sons the invaluable support of family after he was gone. Despite the best medical care, Craig died at home with family near. While our loss is great, we remember with great fondness his warmth and irrepressible exuberance for life.

Hannah Marie Kingsley
November 18, 2004–August 28, 2009

Hannah was born with several heart defects and survived for four and a half years. Hannah was funny, dramatic, and smart. She could be sweet when she wanted to be and tough when she had to be. Hannah had a strength that went beyond her years. She was

happy and enjoyed life. She liked to tease, and it was common to hear Hannah's laugh every few minutes throughout the day. She sang every day.

Hannah was full of life. Being in her presence was like standing in the sun. She radiated love throughout her entire being. To be in Hannah's presence was to truly know joy. She had the ability to touch lives and renew faith in a gentle and loving God. Hannah's life was a gift. Hannah's story is a love from God.

Troy Leonard Juntunen
January 28, 1967–August 3, 2012

Troy was the oldest of our four children. We jokingly called him our "training child." From his earliest years he never did anything halfway! He was optimistic, adventurous, passionate, tolerant, understanding, reliable, trustworthy, kind, compassionate, diligent, resilient, and fun. His Christian faith was an important part of his life, and he was an active member of his church. Troy's bragging rights were many, and his most important was as an actively engaged father of two sons, Eli and Drew. He participated in their school and church activities, coached and supported their sports teams, and was always there for them.

He loved a challenge. He was an avid runner and completed the Tri-Cities Marathon. He participated in the Mud Run and the Dirty Dash Race. He was training for the Tough Mudder Run when he collapsed and died instantly of a heart attack.

Troy was an IT engineer with Battelle Memorial Institute (Pacific Northwest National Laboratories) in Richland, Washington. His colleagues remember him as a "people person," fun-loving, and an avid Oregon State Beaver fan. For his family and friends, he was a caring, loving person. After his death, a friend started a Facebook page, "Remembering Troy." It was comforting and impressive to read about all the lives our son had touched.

Cameron Merrill
September 4, 2010- January 17, 2013

Cameron was a silly, smiley, goofy, fun-loving boy! His smiles totally describe him. He loved *Blue's Clues* and *Go, Diego, Go!*, being outside, and playing in water. He adored his brother, Cressey, and sister, Keylin, who are twins and four years older. He wanted to be big just like them! Cameron was a big kid trapped in a little kid body. He loved to wrestle and play with his brother and be babied by his sister.

He was a people pleaser and just wanted to make everyone happy. Through all of his hard chemo and treatment, he just took it as it came and went with the flow. He was the toughest, bravest person his parents have ever met. He smiled through the tough stuff and just kept going as if it were just a bump in the road.

Jackson McNutt
2008–Present (living with a terminal disease)

In 2012, our son was diagnosed with Duchenne Muscular Dystrophy. Jackson is such a sweet little boy. He not only cares deeply for his family, but he also looks for ways to help the people he meets. Jackson has a love for geography and traveling that is outshone only by an admiration for all things in the animal kingdom.

He has a connection with his mother that is exemplified through after-school activities such as baking, crafting, and researching various subjects on the computer. While Jackson spends much of the day with his mother, he saves his adventurous side for his father. Going to the movies, playing outside, and helping with anything tool-related piques Jackson's interest when it comes to spending time with Dad. While his day-to-day life has become more challenging as time goes on, Jackson has always found the light in any situation he encounters.

Sam Lahr
January 15, 1989–August 2, 2009

Sam loved music, technology, trains, the beach, spending time with friends, playing guitar, attending plays at the Oregon Shakespeare Festival, Disneyland and, and In-N-Out burgers. He had a beautiful singing voice that only a privileged few ever heard. Known online as "SlyOne," Sam was acclaimed for his exceptional computer skills not only with games but also with computer repair and technical support. This ability created a small community of people of all ages who depended on him to keep their computers alive and healthy.

Sam once commented that he was not suited for the way life works. In his uniqueness, this was probably true.

Dallan James Fisher
July 23, 1988–January 14, 1992

Dallan was born the day after his mother Susan's birthday and died the day after his father Scott's. So, obviously, he planned on always being remembered.

Diagnosed at ten months with Wilms' Tumor, he underwent chemotherapy for the rest of his life. But that didn't stop him from living life to the fullest. Full of mischief, he managed to pull off stunts such as emptying any full container he came across, snitching chocolate chips, and baking his bottles. One of the loves of his life was trains. He loved to play with them, and it was a treat for him to go to the tracks nearby and watch them.

With three older siblings (Anjai, Devin, Shann) and one younger (Ky), who loved to play and watch over him, he created memories that will always be special to his family. Dallan holds a special place in our hearts and will always be remembered.

Scott Frederick Merten
November 30, 1973–July 12, 1990

Scott loved hanging out with his friends, playing games with his family, laughing, and keeping his family laughing too.

His attribute of self-confidence without guile endeared him to practically everybody. He had a smile that lit up the room. He was able to implicitly offer acceptance to people while also examining difference or behavior without being threatened by it or necessarily accepting it.

Scott didn't like to match his socks, so he just kept a cardboard box in his closet where he would dump any of his clean socks. In the morning, he just grabbed two socks, not caring if they matched. This sort of became his trademark among his friends. At Scott's funeral, many kids showed us they had worn unmatched socks as a tribute to Scott.

Scott was killed as a passenger in a teenage car crash during the summer of 1990. He has five siblings (Jeff, Eric, Greg, Paul, and Anne), who love and miss him dearly.

Joshua Roland Nelson
October 29, 1992–December 18, 2012

Josh was kind, smart, athletic, and hardworking. He was the second of five children born to Jared and Beth Nelson, and brother of Brad, Andrea, Spencer, and Michael. While a toddler, he discovered Legos and Star Wars, and he enjoyed them throughout his life.

As a young teen, he saved and purchased the Death Star Lego set, and then spent weeks assembling it before putting it on permanent display. He was an Eagle Scout and loved the outdoors. He liked to run, swim, bike, and pole vault. He competed in cross-country, swimming, and track in high school, and several sprint triathlons. He excelled in math and science and was considering majoring in biochemistry.

He died shortly after finishing his third semester of college. At extended family gatherings, Josh was always surrounded by a crowd of admiring younger cousins whom he cheerfully played with.

Megan Elaine Forrest
July 17, 1985–April 19, 2005

Megan was a strong-willed and spirited individual from her birth until her death. Due to a stroke at birth, she was diagnosed with cerebral palsy and left-side weakness. She was willing to try anything and did not let her disabilities slow her down.

She was the oldest of five siblings. After graduating from high school, she was able to get a job at a bakery/restaurant and lived in her own apartment. She was fiercely proud of her independence.

She loved listening to Billy Joel, and her favorite song, "Goodnight, My Angel," was appropriately played at her memorial service. Legos and teddy bears brought her joy also. She died of a seizure disorder at the age of twenty.

Marc David Harris
August 22, 1980–August 14, 1986

Marc was the sixth child of Brent and Janet Harris. He was a joy to his family from the day he was born. He brought a lot of fun, love, and laughter to our home. He so enjoyed all of his brothers and sisters. He especially loved to be with his dad on the lawn tractor. A favorite family photo is of him with a huge smile riding a tractor with his dad. In another photo, he was so sad because he had to get off the tractor.

Marc was in a drowning accident one week before his sixth birthday. Anyone who knew him will always remember him. At reunions, a little picture of Marc is always placed in the corner of the framed family picture. He is still a part of us all. We all still miss him, but we believe we will see him again when we leave this life. What a joyous time it will be for all of us to be together again.

Brooke Carol Wilberger
February 20, 1985–May 24, 2004

Brooke was a happy young woman who was full of life. She grew up in Veneta, Oregon, with her five siblings, and she graduated from Elmira High School in 2003. She had many friends and loved to do things for them. She was always finding ways to lift others. Her favorite song was "Have I Done Any Good in the World Today?"

Brooke began attending Brigham Young University in the fall of 2003. After finishing her first year of college, she began a spring–summer job in Corvallis, Oregon, in April 2004. On a sunny Monday morning, May 24, 2004, Brooke was kidnapped at her work site and murdered. We are grateful for the nineteen years we had together. She holds a special place in our hearts, and we are thankful for the knowledge that families are forever.

Elena Marie Knight
November 14, 2009–April 14, 2010

When I think of my baby Elena, her gifts are what I remember. I had moments when I was stretched thin—weeks of being up with a baby and a toddler most of the night. There were days when I couldn't synchronize their naps and sneak a snooze for myself. But they blended with the days of pure bliss to give me the gift of a perfectly balanced life.

And then I said good-bye. The last time I saw her, I kissed her cheeks and said good-bye, a final loving farewell. I left her with her devoted grandmother, where she died quietly in the early morning of SIDS.

Time has passed, yet her gifts haven't stopped coming. The strength, unity, understanding, and above all, the love she left us—these are lifetime gifts that each day I have the opportunity to receive from my happy, beautiful, lovable daughter.

Lane Anthony Martin
May 1, 1971–April 25, 1982

Lane was an energetic and fun-loving youngster. He was filled with an unconditional acceptance of everyone. He admired and looked up to his brother, Shawn, who was four years older. Even though they had their disputes, they were best friends and loved to be together.

When it came to chores at home, Lane was exceptional at escaping work. He always found other things to do. Though frustrating at the time, now, as I reflect on his short ten years, eleven months, and five days' sojourn on this earth, I am grateful he enjoyed life and skipped the chores. He was generous to a fault, extremely affectionate, and loyal to family and friends. Lane always had something in his pockets to play with and food to eat and share.

Lane was tragically killed in a hanging after playing a "good guy/ bad guy" game with two children about his age. A lot of love and energy dissipated when Lane died. Regrets and guilt filled my life. Time has lessened the pain, but as his mother, I will never "get over" the death of this beloved child.

Lindsay Renee Miller
January 24, 1978–February 7, 1978

After some fertility issues and several miscarriages, my husband, Michael, and I were so blessed to have a healthy pregnancy and welcome our first child, Lindsay Renee Miller.

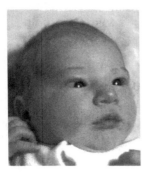

We had no idea that our time with Lindsay would be so short. After contracting an upper respiratory illness, she died from complications of pneumonia at just two weeks of age. Though we did not get to hold her in our arms for very long, she will always be close in our hearts.

As young heartbroken parents, we thought we would never heal. We threw ourselves into work and service to others and held on to our faith and each other.

Lynette Lorane Miller
November 17, 1981–September 15, 2011

Lynette was our spunky and beautiful princess. Her family called her "Netty," but to her many, much-beloved friends, who were such an important part of her life, she was "Lynny." Her favorite color was yellow, and one of her nicknames was "Sunshine Girl." She brightened every room she entered and could make anyone laugh, whether stranger or friend.

Lynette was always the center of attention (which was just how she liked it). She always spoke her mind, and you never doubted where she was coming from. Lynette took great pleasure in caring for others, both people and animals alike. She displayed strength for the world to see, deliberately masking her vulnerability. She was a loyal friend, a talented artist, a creative writer, and an inventive chef.

Lynette will be forever remembered for her vibrant, creative, joyous, and generous spirit. Her favorite quote was from the late actor James Dean: "Dream as if you'll live forever. Live as if you'll die today." Lynette cherished us, and she will always be cherished in our hearts.

Her parents; siblings Carynn, Bret, and Melinda; and nieces and nephews survive Lynette. Her oldest sister, Lindsay, passed away as an infant. Lynette died from alcohol poisoning.

Alex Newport-Berra
June 14, 1981–July 20, 2014

Alex Newport-Berra left us doing what he loved in the midst of the beauty and majesty of the Rocky Mountains of Colorado. He lived every day, every hour, and, indeed, every minute to its fullest, taking in the joy, beauty, wonder, and magic of everyone and everything around him.

Always an explorer, his adventures began in the Willamette Valley and inspired him to see nature's beauty in places like Hawaii, Montana, Colorado, Italy, and Costa Rica. Each journey was accompanied by sport, and no matter which sport he embraced—climbing, running, cycling, yoga, surfing, skiing, or hiking—he did it with focus, passion, and a respect for and love of nature.

He was and continues to be a gifted and compassionate teacher. He listened and learned from those he inspired and mentored. He empowered youth and adults alike with his philosophy captured in one of his quotes, "May each pilot their own ship, and may your life's passion be a wind to fill other's sails."

Alex was a writer and storyteller. Anyone can sense his infinite wisdom blended with an uncanny and youthful naïveté at his blog: alexnberra.wordpress.com.

PERSONAL THOUGHTS
AND NOTES

— ❀ —

ABOUT THE AUTHORS

Nikki M. King is the mother of five children. Nikki writes about loss from firsthand experience. Her younger brother died when she was sixteen and she remembers the grief vividly. She then lost her beloved daughter Taylor as a young mother. During the grieving process, writing became her personal therapeutic outlet which led to her coauthoring this book. Her goal is that these words will bring hope and inspiration to parents who have lost a child. Nikki currently resides in Corvallis, Oregon, with her husband, Eric, and their four living children.

Coauthoring a book for parents who have lost a child was not on Alice Rampton's "bucket list." When her daughter Lora died in 1986, she joined that unique group of parents who view the world through a different lens. Children are not supposed to die before their parents. And when they do, one's world is turned upside down.

Reading and journaling were cathartic at the time of Lora's death, but both Alice and her physician husband felt that another great resource came from dialogue with other parents who had experienced loss. She and Nikki King wrote this book with a common goal of bringing peace and comfort into the hearts of anyone who is going through the grieving process.

Three decades after Lora's death, she can assure the reader that "it" will get better.